HUMAN RIGHTS

**GREAT
SPEECHES
IN
HISTORY**

Laura Hitt, *Book Editor*

Daniel Leone, *President*

Bonnie Szumski, *Publisher*

Scott Barbour, *Managing Editor*

Greenhaven Press, Inc.
San Diego, California

Library of Congress Cataloging-in-Publication Data

Human rights / Laura Hitt, book editor.
p. cm. — (Greenhaven Press's great speeches in history)
Includes bibliographical references and index.
ISBN 0-7377-0874-3 (pbk. : alk. paper) —
ISBN 0-7377-0875-1 (lib. : alk. paper) —
1. Human rights. I. Hitt, Laura. II. Greenhaven Press great speeches in history.

JC571 .H686 2002
323—dc21

2001050175

Cover Photo: © Bettmann/Corbis
Library of Congress, 15
National Archives, 111, 141

© 2002 by Greenhaven Press, Inc.
10911 Technology Place
San Diego, CA 92127

Printed in the U.S.A.

Contents

the Burmese as well as women and children in her political efforts.

Chapter 2: The Right to Free Speech and Worship

importance of religious freedom for Cubans as well as economic and social justice for Cuba as a member of the international community.

Chapter 3: Equal Rights: Emancipation for All

Chapter 4: Human Rights: An International Responsibility

ual slavery, protecting the human rights of the victims must be the first priority.

Foreword

I have a dream that one day this nation will rise up and live out the true meaning of its creed: "We hold these truths to be self-evident: that all men are created equal."

I have a dream that one day on the red hills of Georgia the sons of former slaves and the sons of former slave owners will be able to sit down together at the table of brotherhood.

I have a dream that one day even the state of Mississippi, a state sweltering with the heat of injustice, sweltering with the heat of oppression, will be transformed into an oasis of freedom and justice.

I have a dream that my four little children will one day live in a nation where they will not be judged by the color of their skin but by the content of their character.

Perhaps no speech in American history resonates as deeply as Martin Luther King Jr.'s "I Have a Dream," delivered in 1963 before a rapt audience of 250,000 on the steps of the Lincoln Memorial in Washington, D.C. Decades later, the speech still enthralls those who read or hear it, and stands as a philosophical guidepost for contemporary discourse on racism.

What distinguishes "I Have a Dream" from the hundreds of other speeches given during the civil rights era are King's eloquence, lyricism, and use of vivid metaphors to convey abstract ideas. Moreover, "I Have a Dream" serves not only as a record of history—a testimony to the racism that permeated American society during the 1960s—but it is also a historical event in its own right. King's speech, aired live on national television, marked the first time that the grave injustice of racism was fully articulated to a mass audience in a way that was both logical and evocative. Julian Bond, a fellow participant in the civil rights movement and student of King's, states that

> King's dramatic 1963 "I Have a Dream" speech before the Lincoln Memorial cemented his place as first among equals in civil rights leadership; from this first televised mass meeting, an American audience saw and heard the unedited oratory of America's finest preacher, and for the first time, a mass white audience heard the undeniable justice of black demands.

Moreover, by helping people to understand the justice of the civil rights movement's demands, King's speech helped to transform the nation. In 1964, a year after the speech was delivered, President Lyndon B. Johnson signed the Civil Rights Act, which outlawed segregation in public facilities and discrimination in employment. In 1965, Congress passed the Voting Rights Act, which forbids restrictions, such as literacy tests, that were commonly used in the South to prevent blacks from voting. King's impact on the country's laws illustrates the power of speech to bring about real change.

Greenhaven Press's Great Speeches in History series offers students an opportunity to read and study some of the greatest speeches ever delivered before an audience. Each volume traces a specific historical era, event, or theme through speeches—both famous and lesser known. An introductory essay sets the stage by presenting background and context. Then a collection of speeches follows, grouped in chapters based on chronology or theme. Each selection is preceded by a brief introduction that offers historical context, biographical information about the speaker, and analysis of the speech. A comprehensive index and an annotated table of contents help readers quickly locate material of interest, and a bibliography serves as a launching point for further research. Finally, an appendix of author biographies provides detailed background on each speaker's life and work. Taken together, the volumes in the Greenhaven Great Speeches in History series offer students vibrant illustrations of history and demonstrate the potency of the spoken word. By reading speeches in their historical context, students will be transported back in time and gain a deeper understanding of the issues that confronted people of the past.

Introduction

The United Nations (UN)—an international organization formed after World War II to ensure worldwide peace, security, and human welfare—works to protect fundamental human rights around the world. The organization is guided by the Universal Declaration of Human Rights (UDHR), which was formally adopted in 1948. This document defines the term *human rights* and sets the standard for protecting those rights worldwide.

The declaration has its roots in a 1941 speech made by then-president Franklin D. Roosevelt, who spoke of Nazi human rights violations during World War II and identified what he believed to be four basic human freedoms: freedom of expression, freedom to worship, freedom from want, and freedom from fear. Expanding on Roosevelt's vision, the UDHR encourages respect for "the highest aspirations of the common people, . . . faith in fundamental human rights, in the dignity and worth of the human person, [and] in the equal rights of men and women and of all nations large and small." It guarantees "human rights and fundamental freedoms for all [people] without distinction as to race, sex, language, or religion."

More specifically, the declaration affirms the right to equal protection against discrimination, arbitrary arrest or exile, slavery, and cruel or inhumane punishment. It also spells out the right to equal opportunity under the law; a fair trial; privacy; the freedom of residence and movement within a home country; political asylum; the freedom to marry without restriction of race, nationality, or religion; and the freedom to own property. Further articles affirm the universal right to freedom of thought, conscience, religion, opinion, speech, assembly, and participation in one's own government.

The adoption of the declaration by the UN was an important step to ensure human rights worldwide, but enforcing these rights has proven difficult. The UN has found it impossible to make some of its member nations strictly adhere to its human rights code. One problem is that, traditionally, the UN has been limited to passive enforcement means such as imposing economic sanctions. Another problem—for some, a very serious one—is that the UDHR's definition of *human rights* is not shared by all nations. According to historian Claude E. Welck, several governments have argued that "human rights as defined in post World War II treaties . . . reflect the basic values of Western democratic, industrialized states and hence [are] not truly global." Leaders of many non-Western and developing nations assert that universal human rights standards do not reflect the needs of their populations or the social and economic agendas of their governments.

Origins of the Concept of Human Rights

Indeed, the concept of human rights did evolve within the Western European and North American traditions of natural rights and liberal individualism. One of the first documents to recognize the concept that humans had innate rights was the Magna Carta, the great charter of English political and civil liberties granted by King John at Runnymede on June 15, 1215. By issuing the charter, King John placed himself and all of England's future sovereigns under a rule of law. For example, kings and magistrates could no longer imprison people arbitrarily; they had to guarantee each person who was arrested a fair trial. The charter guarantees that "no freeman shall be taken, imprisoned, . . . or in any other way destroyed . . . except by the lawful judgment of his peers, or by the law of the land." The Magna Carta has served as a model for political leaders—such as the founders of the U.S. Constitution—seeking to establish a law code that guarantees citizens' basic rights.

Whereas the Magna Carta guaranteed the protection of

certain rights by law, the writings of seventeenth-century English philosopher John Locke expressed the idea of natural rights—that is, rights innate to human beings apart from law or custom. Locke argued, in effect, that nature had endowed human beings with inalienable rights that could not be usurped by any governing authority. Locke also proposed that sovereignty resided with the people rather than with the state and that governments were obligated to protect the rights of individuals.

Such ideas about rights were further articulated in two late-eighteenth-century manifestos: the U.S. Bill of Rights and the French Declaration of the Rights of Man and Citizen. These documents enumerate a number of rights to which all are entitled, including the right to life, liberty, and property; the right to participate in politics and government; and the right to due process and equal protection under the law. They also establish freedom of religion, freedom of speech, and freedom of assembly. These two documents greatly influenced political thought in the nineteenth and twentieth centuries and became models for many of the world's modern democracies.

The term *human rights* itself was first coined by American writer Henry David Thoreau in his treatise "Civil Disobedience." The phrase replaced the terms *natural rights* and *rights of man* and entered into general usage following World War II, after the creation of the United Nations. One of the advantages of the phrase *human rights* is that it suggests universal applicability. Indeed, the groups most affected by modern human rights violations worldwide include people whom early philosophers such as Locke—living in societies where only white men were recognized as citizens—may not have envisioned as having "natural rights." For example, the UN currently works to stop discrimination against women—who were not citizens in Locke's time. In general, groups affected by human rights violations are the disenfranchised everywhere: ethnic, political, and religious minorities; indigenous people; slaves; refugees; and the poor. The rights of workers have also been a focus of human rights campaigns. In all cases, the individuals who belong to these groups are at the mercy of powers that do not recognize their rights, as defined in the Western tradition. Violations of their rights include ethnic cleansing (the process of removing one ethnic group of people from their homes by another group), torture, discrimination, forced labor, forced prostitution, and arbitrary imprisonment.

Human rights violations have been a long-standing international concern. Many of the most serious human rights violations have their roots in imperialism—the policy of extending a nation's authority by territorial acquisition or by the establishment of economic and political hegemony over other nations. Classic Western imperialism began during the fifteenth century when the Dutch and Portuguese began to colonize new lands. During the late fifteenth century, the Spanish began to colonize the New World, and explorers such as Christopher Columbus were encouraged by their government to take as many riches—diamonds, gold, gems—as possible from the new lands and to establish colonies. The French and British began imperialist expansion during the eighteenth century. Unfortunately, while often bringing riches and prestige to conquering empires, imperialism more often than not resulted in the oppression of the conquered. Colonists often thought of the native people as savages because they practiced different religions and customs, and the colonists used such condemnation to justify their attempts to subdue the natives by enslavement, religious conversion, or war.

Fighting Against Oppression

Violations of human rights such as those that occurred as a result of imperialism seem to be part of the human condition, but so too do efforts to fight against oppression. Two twentieth-century examples of racial discrimination—in the United States and South Africa—illustrate both the historical roots of oppression and the will and courage of those who oppose it. In both cases, imperialism was the force that caused the oppression to take root and grow, and in both cases, a leader emerged who inspired others to fight the injustice. Although both leaders were successful in gaining rights for their people, their methods of achieving similar ends were very different.

One of the most influential civil rights leaders in the world,

Martin Luther King Jr., was an ordained minister with a doctorate in theology. King led the 1960s American civil rights movement to overthrow laws that enforced segregation, especially in the South. Racism in America was deeply entrenched, beginning when the first slaves were brought to the New World from Africa by the English colonists. Although the Thirteenth Amendment to the U.S. Constitution had outlawed slavery, discrimination against blacks continued unabated. Many laws in the South, for example, prohibited blacks from sharing lunch counters with whites or sitting in certain sections of buses. In addition, blacks were often prevented from voting by special poll taxes and literacy tests. Clearly, conditions in the United States at this time constituted a violation of human rights as enumerated in the United Nations Declaration of Human Rights, especially the right to equal protection against discrimination.

Against this backdrop, King tried to forge a just society. Trained as a preacher, he developed into a brilliant orator and was able to convince many people to adopt his views. In his famous "I Have a Dream" speech, the civil rights leader

As the leader of the 1960s American civil rights movement, Martin Luther King Jr. organized nonviolent protests against laws that enforced segregation.

helped articulate the movement's goals: "I have a dream that my four children will one day live in a nation where they will not be judged by the color of their skin but by the content of their character."

King became famous for organizing nonviolent protests against unfair and unconstitutional laws, and in 1964, he was awarded the Nobel Peace Prize in recognition of his efforts. His advocacy of nonviolent resistance, which was inspired by the tenets of Indian leader Mohandas Gandhi, in turn served as a model for future activists. Like many fervent advocates of human rights, King was willing to sacrifice for the advancement of his cause. He was arrested many times for participating in nonviolent protests, his life was often threatened, and his home was bombed. However, in spite of the abuses he suffered, he and his followers never retaliated with violence. Unfortunately, like many leaders before him, King paid the ultimate price for his activism. In Memphis, Tennessee, on April 4, 1968, King was assassinated. Before he died, however, the great leader was able to see that his actions had made a difference. Led by King, the American civil rights movement helped change attitudes in the South and spur legislation that has benefited all Americans. According to English professor Lee Jacobus, King "became famous as a man who stood for human rights and human dignity virtually everywhere."

At the same time on the other side of the world, segregation was institutionalized by law in South Africa. This official policy of racial segregation—called apartheid—established separate residential and business districts for blacks, who were the native majority, and whites, who were descendants of English colonizers. Under this regime, the white minority had all the power. For instance, although only 4.5 million whites occupied South Africa in 1978 compared to 19 million blacks, whites owned 87 percent of the land and earned 75 percent of the national income. Laws passed in the 1950s established separate public facilities for whites and nonwhites and required blacks to carry passbooks so that the government could regulate their travel through the country. Perhaps most serious, under apartheid, blacks could not vote. The conditions in South Africa violated several clauses

of the UDHR, including the right to participation in government and freedom of residence; as a result, the United Nations imposed economic sanctions against the nation.

In 1944, a young lawyer named Nelson Mandela helped
establish the African National Congress Youth League,
which advocated boycotts, strikes, civil disobedience, and
noncooperation with the government in order to obtain full
citizenship and direct parliamentary representation for all
South Africans. During the 1950s, Mandela was frequently
arrested for participating in nonviolent protests. In spite of
government persecution, Mandela continued to advise his
followers to adopt a peaceful course of action and to avoid
all violence. During the 1960s, however, Mandela and his
followers changed tactics. After assessing the situation in
South Africa, they decided that "as violence in [South Africa]
was inevitable, it would be wrong and unrealistic for African
leaders to continue preaching peace and nonviolence at a
time when the government met our peaceful demands with
force. It was only when all else had failed, when all channels
of peaceful protest had been barred to us, that the decision
was made to embark on violent forms of political struggle.
. . . The Government had left us no other choice."

Throughout the 1960s and '70s, violent demonstrations
and student riots broke out across South Africa to protest the
government's racist policies. Mandela and his organization
helped orchestrate many of the protests. The internal pressure this produced, in conjunction with international protests
against the situation in South Africa, helped weaken support
for the reigning government. On June 12, 1964, Mandela
was convicted of sabotage and trying to overthrow the government and was sentenced to life in prison. During his
twenty-six-year prison term, Mandela rejected all offers of
early release. In the 1980s, for example, he rejected an offer
of release on the condition that he renounce violence. He argued that prisoners could not enter into contracts, that only
free men can negotiate. Mandela was released from prison on
February 11, 1990, during the presidency of F.W. de Klerk,
who—under international and domestic pressure—was
working to repeal many of the nation's most discriminatory
laws. In 1994, Mandela defeated de Klerk in the nation's first

universal suffrage election and became president of South
Africa. Mandela continued to work for equality even after
leaving office in 1999.

For many, Mandela symbolizes the triumph of the human
spirit over man's inhumanity to man. As with Martin Luther
King Jr., Mandela's work fighting for human rights was internationally recognized when he won the Nobel Peace Prize
in 1993. Also like King, Mandela was prepared to suffer for
the cause of human rights. At one of his trials, he stated, "I
have fought against white domination, and I have fought
against black domination. I have cherished the ideal of a
democratic and free society in which all persons live together
in harmony and with equal opportunities. It is an ideal which
I hope to live for and to achieve. But if need be, it is an ideal
for which I am prepared to die."

International Efforts

Controversies over perceived violations of human rights have
raged for centuries and have produced great activists such as
King and Mandela who were willing to sacrifice—even die—
to further freedom and equality. What exactly human rights
are has been hotly debated, and such debates did not subside
when the United Nations published its Universal Declaration
of Human Rights. As the UN found, it is difficult to force
foreign governments to adhere to international standards of
human rights when those governments do not deem recognition of such rights as beneficial to their regimes. A fact that
amply illustrates this difficulty is that the United States and
South Africa were both members of the United Nations at
the time that King and Mandela were fighting against racial
discrimination. Clearly, non-Western nations such as China
who do not share the Western roots of many UN members
can prove to be even more intractable. Often, the UN has
had to settle for sustaining a nation's suffering people by de-
livering food and medicine to them as opposed to effecting
change in the way their governments conduct business.

Recognizing the limitations of the UN, many nongovernment organizations such as Amnesty International have
stepped in to help monitor human rights abuses worldwide.

Amnesty International works to free people detained for their beliefs and people imprisoned because of their ethnic origin, sex, language, national or social origin, economic status, or birth. Human Rights Watch is another organization that regularly investigates human rights abuses in more than seventy countries around the world. It promotes civil liberties and defends freedom of thought, due process, and the equal protection of the law. Despite the efforts of government and nongovernment entities, however, human rights violations continue.

No matter how difficult it is to come up with a universally accepted definition of *human rights* or to enforce them once defined, individuals throughout time and from all over the world seem to have had an innate sense of when their dignity as a human being is being violated. Throughout history, too, individuals have been willing to fight for their dignity against unfair systems: A slaughterhouse worker organizes a union, a slave stages an uprising, a woman registers for classes at an all-male college. Helping these individuals obtain their rights, the great speech makers have addressed those in power, those suffering, and those upholding the status quo. They call upon governments to enact fair laws and enforce those laws. The orators call out to the disenfranchised, urging them to protest and organize. Finally, the great leaders speak to those who do not suffer under unjust regimes, who are not oppressed, and ask them to support the rights of others in order to protect their own freedom. In the words of Martin Luther King Jr., "Injustice anywhere is a threat to justice everywhere. We are caught in an inescapable network of mutuality, tied in a single garment of destiny."

CHAPTER
ONE

The Foundation of Human Rights: The People vs. Ruling Powers

"Cast Off the Yoke of Bondage"

John Ball

During England's Middle Ages, the clergy and nobility ruled. However, rumblings of change emerged following two events: the Black Death, which hit England in 1348–1349, 1362, and 1369; and the movement of John Wycliffe (1324–1384). An Oxford professor, Wycliffe declared that the first Christians had lived in devout poverty and attacked the priests of the Catholic Church for their lavish ways, concluding that everybody within the Church should live as modestly as the first Christians.

With the population considerably diminished by the plague, many peasants began to appreciate the power they could wield. As a result they felt the strength to speak up and oppose unfair demands made by King Richard, local nobility, and clergymen. The Peasants' Revolt of 1381, one of the earliest recorded revolts of the English peasantry, originated from the peasant's opposition to a poll tax of one shilling imposed by Parliament on any man or woman fifteen years or older. (The average peasant's wage during that time was twelve shillings a year.) Indignation, outrage, and eventually rebellion ensued. This event was one of the most organized revolts against the authority of the monarchy to dictate law and one of the first attempts of a people to object to the dictates of a ruler.

Wat Tyler was the man who led the charge. However, it was itinerant peasant priest John Ball who inspired the protesters. Although supported by Wycliffe, Ball had been excommunicated in 1376 for his advocacy of "ecclesiasti-

---

From a speech delivered by John Ball at Blackheath, England, on June 13, 1381.

cal poverty and social equality" for priests, a philosophy opposed by powerful clergy. Just prior to the revolt, the bishop of Canterbury imprisoned Ball for continuing to espouse his ideas.

On June 10, 1381, peasants began to march toward London to protest the unfair taxation. On their way, the rebels liberated prisoners from prisons kept by the clergy and nobility. John Ball, one of those freed prisoners, was an important addition to the cause. He contributed his enthusiasm and reputation as a priest who stood for social equity and change as well as inspiring oratorical skills. On June 13, his speech energized thousands of peasants to continue their march toward London. Soon thereafter soldiers captured and tried him for treason. He was sentenced to be hanged, drawn, and quartered, a typical sentence for traitors, and was executed on June 15, 1381.

From the beginning all men by nature were created alike, and our bondage or servitude came in by the unjust oppression of naughty men. For if God would have had any bondmen from the beginning, he would have appointed who should be bond, and who free. And therefore I exhort you to consider that now the time is come, appointed to us by God, in which ye may (if ye will) cast off the yoke of bondage, and recover liberty. I counsel you therefore well to bethink yourselves, and to take good hearts unto you, that after the manner of a good husband that tilleth his ground, and riddeth out thereof such evil weeds as choke and destroy the good corn, you may destroy first the great lords of the realm, and after, the judges and lawyers, and questmongers, and all other who have undertaken to be against the commons. For so shall you procure peace and surety to yourselves in time to come; and by dispatching out of the way the great men, there shall be an equality in liberty, and no difference in degrees of nobility; but a like dignity and equal authority in all things brought in among you.

"Give Me Liberty or Give Me Death!"

Patrick Henry

Patrick Henry was a Virginian who struggled in business and eventually studied law. Elected to the Virginia House of Burgesses at the age of twenty-nine, he gained attention for his resolutions against the Stamp Act. In 1776, he would become the governor of the state. Known as a fiery orator, Henry delivered his greatest speech during the second Virginia revolutionary convention in 1775. In it he supported the resolution calling for colonies to place themselves on alert to the aggression of the British. This speech, recognized as one of the most brilliant discourses of the pre-Revolutionary period in America, turned the tide toward the Revolution. Henry uses inflammatory language to call on the Continental Congress to take action by uniting against English colonial policies. The impact of this speech was so powerful that the Constitutional Congress acted immediately to pass the resolutions for defense against further aggression by the British.

After the Revolutionary War, while the Constitution was being drafted, divisive lines were drawn between the Federalists, who wanted a strong central government, and Anti-Federalists, who favored a weaker central government. Despite his earlier efforts to unite the colonies against England, Henry refused to attend the Philadelphia Constitutional Convention and led the Anti-Federalist opposition to ratification of the Constitution. He became a persuasive advocate for the Bill of Rights, the first ten amendments to the Constitution that outlined the rights specifically protected from government intrusion.

From Patrick Henry's speech delivered to the Virginia Convention of Delegates, March 28, 1775.

No man thinks more highly than I do of the patriotism, as well as abilities, of the very worthy gentlemen who have just addressed the House. But different men often see the same subject in different lights; and, therefore, I hope it will not be thought disrespectful to those gentlemen if, entertaining as I do opinions of a character very opposite to theirs, I shall speak forth my sentiments freely and without reserve. This is no time for ceremony. The question before the House is one of awful moment to this country. For my own part, I consider it as nothing less than a question of freedom or slavery; and in proportion to the magnitude of the subject ought to be the freedom of the debate. It is only in this way that we can hope to arrive at truth, and fulfill the great responsibility which we hold to God and our country. Should I keep back my opinions at such a time, through fear of giving offense, I should consider myself as guilty of treason towards my country, and of an act of disloyalty toward the Majesty of Heaven, which I revere above all earthly kings.

Mr. President, it is natural to man to indulge in the illusions of hope. We are apt to shut our eyes against a painful truth, and listen to the song of that siren till she transforms us into beasts. Is this the part of wise men, engaged in a great and arduous struggle for liberty? Are we disposed to be of the number of those who, having eyes, see not, and, having ears, hear not, the things which so nearly concern their temporal salvation? For my part, whatever anguish of spirit it may cost, I am willing to know the whole truth; to know the worst, and to provide for it.

We Must Fight

I have but one lamp by which my feet are guided, and that is the lamp of experience. I know of no way of judging of the future but by the past. And judging by the past, I wish to know what there has been in the conduct of the British ministry for the last ten years to justify those hopes with which gentlemen have been pleased to solace themselves and the House. Is it that insidious smile with which our petition has been lately received? Trust it not, sir; it will prove a snare to your feet. Suffer not yourselves to be betrayed with a kiss. Ask yourselves how this gracious reception of our petition comports with those warlike preparations which cover our waters and darken our land. Are fleets and armies necessary to a work of love and reconciliation? Have we shown ourselves so unwilling to be reconciled that force must be called in to win back our love? Let us not deceive ourselves, sir. These are the implements of war and subjugation; the last arguments to which kings resort. I ask gentlemen, sir, what means this martial array, if its purpose be not to force us to submission? Can gentlemen assign any other possible motive for it? Has Great Britain any enemy, in this quarter of the world, to call for all this accumulation of navies and armies? No, sir, she has none. They are meant for us: they can be meant for no other. They are sent over to bind and rivet upon us those chains which the British ministry have been so long forging. And what have we to oppose to them? Shall we try argument? Sir, we have been trying that for the last ten years. Have we anything new to offer upon the subject? Nothing. We have held the subject up in every light of which it is capable; but it has been all in vain. Shall we resort to entreaty and humble supplication? What terms shall we find which have not been already exhausted? Let us not, I beseech you, sir, deceive ourselves. Sir, we have done everything that could be done to avert the storm which is now coming on. We have petitioned; we have remonstrated; we have supplicated; we have prostrated ourselves before the throne, and have implored its interposition to arrest the tyrannical hands of the ministry and Parliament. Our petitions have been slighted; our remonstrances have produced additional violence and insult; our supplications have been disregarded; and we have been spurned, with contempt, from the foot of the throne! In vain, after these things, may we indulge the fond hope of peace and reconciliation. There is no longer any room for hope. If we wish to be free—if we mean to preserve inviolate those inestimable privileges for which we have been so long contending—if we mean not basely to abandon the noble struggle in which we have been so long engaged, and which we have pledged ourselves never to abandon until the glorious object of our contest shall be obtained—we must fight! I repeat it, sir, we must fight! An appeal to arms and to the God of hosts is all that is left us!

The Holy Cause of Liberty

They tell us, sir, that we are weak; unable to cope with so formidable an adversary. But when shall we be stronger? Will it be the next week, or the next year? Will it be when we are totally disarmed, and when a British guard shall be stationed in every house? Shall we gather strength by irresolution and inaction? Shall we acquire the means of effectual resistance by lying supinely on our backs and hugging the delusive phantom of hope, until our enemies shall have bound us hand and foot? Sir, we are not weak if we make a proper use of those means which the God of nature hath placed in our power. The millions of people, armed in the holy cause of liberty, and in such a country as that which we possess, are invincible by any force which our enemy can send against us. Besides, sir, we shall not fight our battles alone. There is a just God who presides over the destinies of nations, and who will raise up friends to fight our battles for us. The battle, sir, is not to the strong alone; it is to the vigilant, the active, the brave. Besides, sir, we have no election. If we were base enough to desire it, it is now too late to retire from the contest. There is no retreat but in submission and slavery! Our chains are forged! Their clanking may be heard on the plains of Boston! The war is inevitable—and let it come! I repeat it, sir, let it come.

It is in vain, sir, to extenuate the matter. Gentlemen may cry, Peace, Peace—but there is no peace. The war is actually begun! The next gale that sweeps from the north will bring to our ears the clash of resounding arms! Our brethren are already in the field! Why stand we here idle? What is it that gentlemen wish? What would they have? Is life so dear, or peace so sweet, as to be purchased at the price of chains and slavery? Forbid it, Almighty God! I know not what course others may take; but as for me, give me liberty or give me death!

Opposition to the Harms of British Rule

Mohandas K. Gandhi

Mohandas K. Gandhi, a native of India and a lawyer by profession, experienced racial discrimination while a law student in England and as a legal consultant in British South Africa. In 1893, while still in South Africa, he decided to fight these racial prejudices. He founded the Natal Indian Congress to fight for Indian rights and became a leader of a South African movement devoted to abolishing discriminatory laws in South Africa. In response to laws that discriminated against Asians, Gandhi adopted a Hindi term, *satyagraha*, meaning "truth force," as the foundation of his philosophy of nonviolent noncooperation with British imperial rule.

Gandhi returned to India in 1915 and began to take up the cause of finding a peaceful means of freeing India from British rule. In 1919, at a peaceful celebration of spring at Amritsar, Punjab, British troops fired on an unarmed crowd of men, women, and children, killing over four hundred people. Gandhi organized the nonviolent noncooperation movement in response to the failure of the British government to take adequate action against those responsible for the Amritsar massacre. Later that year he became the editor of *Young India,* a publication that was to become an influential vehicle for his views on Indian home rule, or *swaraj.*

In 1922 Gandhi was arrested and charged with sedition for articles published in *Young India.* The following

From Mohandas K. Gandhi's statement at his trial for sedition in Madras, India, March 23, 1922.

speech is excerpted from the statement he made. Gandhi defends his opposition to British rule of India, declaring that the British system has oppressed and brutalized the Indian people while promised reforms have failed to materialize. Gandhi freely admits that he has broken the law by promoting disaffection toward the government and implores the judge to impose the maximum sentence. Because the law is unjust and is used to oppress dissent, Gandhi maintains, he considers it "a privilege" to be charged under it. By taking this stance, Gandhi dramatically and effectively criticizes the system of British rule even while suffering under its weight. After giving the speech, Gandhi was convicted to six years of imprisonment. Due to an appendicitis attack and political pressures, he was released two years later in 1924.

Gandhi's philosophy of using nonviolence in the struggle for political change has had a profound influence on the philosophies and actions of many political, civil, and human rights leaders throughout the world, including Martin Luther King Jr., Nelson Mandela, and Daw Aung San Suu Kyi.

I would like to state that I entirely endorse the learned advocate general's remarks in connection with my humble self. I think that he was entirely fair to me in all the statements that he has made, because it is very true, and I have no desire whatsoever to conceal from this court the fact that to preach disaffection toward the existing system of government has become almost a passion with me; and the learned advocate general is also entirely in the right when he says that my preaching of disaffection did not commence with my connection with *Young India,* but that it commenced much earlier. . . . I wish to endorse all the blame that the learned advocate general has thrown on my shoulders, in connection with the Bombay occurrences, Madras occurrences, and the Chauri Chaura occurrences [in which protests turned violent]. Thinking over these deeply and sleeping over them night after night, it is impossible for me to dissociate myself from the diabolical crimes of Chauri Chaura or the mad outrages of Bombay. He is quite right when he says that as a man of responsibility, a man having received a fair share of education, having had a fair share of experience of this world, I should have known the consequences of every one of my acts. I know that I was playing with fire. I ran the risk, and if I was set free, I would still do the same. I have felt it this morning that I would have failed in my duty, if I did not say what I said here just now.

I wanted to avoid violence, I want to avoid violence. Nonviolence is the first article of my faith. It is also the last article of my creed. But I had to make my choice. I had either to submit to a system which I considered had done an irreparable harm to my country, or incur the risk of the mad fury of my people bursting forth, when they understood the truth from my lips. I know that my people have sometimes gone mad. I am deeply sorry for it, and I am therefore here to submit not to a light penalty but to the highest penalty. I do not ask for mercy. I do not plead any extenuating act. I am here, therefore, to invite and cheerfully submit to the highest penalty that can be inflicted upon me for what in law is a deliberate crime and what appears to me to be the highest duty of a citizen. The only course open to you, the judge, is . . . either to resign your post or inflict on me the severest penalty, if you believe that the system and law you are assisting to administer are good for the people. I do not expect that kind of conversation, but by the time I have finished with my statement, you will perhaps have a glimpse of what is raging within my breast to run this maddest risk which a sane man can run.

I owe it perhaps to the Indian public and to the public in England to placate which this prosecution is mainly taken up that I should explain why from a staunch loyalist and cooperator I have become an uncompromising disaffectionist and non-cooperator. To the court too I should say why I plead guilty to the charge of promoting disaffection toward the government established by law in India.

My public life began in 1893 in South Africa in troubled weather. My first contact with British authority in that country was not of a happy character. I discovered that as a man and as an Indian I had no rights. More correctly, I discovered that I had no rights as a man because I was an Indian.

But I was not baffled. I thought that this treatment of Indians was an excrescence upon a system that was intrinsically and mainly good. I gave the government my voluntary and hearty cooperation, criticizing it freely where I felt it was faulty but never wishing its destruction.

Consequently, when the existence of the empire was threatened in 1899 by the Boer challenge, I offered my services to it, raised a volunteer ambulance corps, and served at several actions that took place for the relief of Ladysmith. Similarly in 1906, at the time of the Zulu revolt, I raised a stretcher-bearer party and served till the end of the "rebellion." On both these occasions I received medals and was even mentioned in dispatches. For my work in South Africa I was given by Lord Hardinge a Kaiser-i-Hind Gold Medal. . . . In all these efforts at service I was actuated by the belief that it was possible by such services to gain a status of full equality in the empire for my countrymen.

The first shock came in the shape of the Rowlatt Act, a law designed to rob the people of all real freedom. I felt called upon to lead an intensive agitation against it. Then followed the Punjab horrors beginning with the [1919] massacre at Jallianwala Bagh and culminating in crawling orders, public floggings, and other indescribable humiliations. I discovered too that the plighted word of the prime minister to the Mussulmans of India regarding the integrity of Turkey and the holy places of Islam was not likely to be fulfilled. But in spite of the forebodings and the grave warnings of friends, at the Amritsar Congress in 1919, I fought for cooperation and working with the Montagu-Chelmsford reforms [named for Edwin S. Montagu, India's secretary of state, and viceroy Lord Chelmsford], hoping that the prime minister would redeem his promise to the Indian Mussulmans, that the Punjab wound would be healed, and that the reforms, inadequate and unsatisfactory though they were, marked a new era of hope in the life of India.

But all that hope was shattered. The Khilafat promise was not to be redeemed. The Punjab crime was whitewashed, and most culprits went not only unpunished but remained in service and in some cases continued to draw pensions from the Indian revenue, and in some cases were even rewarded. I saw too that not only did the reforms not mark a change of heart, but they were only a method of further draining India of her wealth and of prolonging her servitude.

The Exploitation of the Masses

I came reluctantly to the conclusion that the British connection had made India more helpless than she ever was before, politically and economically. A disarmed India has no power of resistance against any aggressor if she wanted to engage in an armed conflict with him. So much is this the case that some of our best men consider that India must take generations before she can achieve the dominion status. She has become so poor that she has little power of resisting famines. Before the British advent, India spun and wove in her millions of cottages just the supplement she needed for adding to her meager agricultural resources. This cottage industry, so vital for India's existence, has been ruined by incredibly heartless and inhuman processes as described by English witnesses. Little do town dwellers know how the semistarved masses of India are slowly sinking to lifelessness. Little do they know that their miserable comfort represents the brokerage they get for the work they do for the foreign exploiter, that the profits and the brokerage are sucked from the masses. Little do they realize that the government established by law in British India is carried on for this exploitation of the masses. No sophistry, no jugglery in figures can explain away the evidence that the skeletons in many villages present to the naked eye. I have no doubt whatsoever that both England and the town dwellers of India will have to answer, if there is a God above, for this crime against humanity which is perhaps unequaled in history. The law itself in this country has been used to serve the foreign exploiter. . . .

The greatest misfortune is that Englishmen and their Indian associates in the administration of the country do not know that they are engaged in the crime I have attempted to describe. I am satisfied that many Englishmen and Indian officials honestly believe that they are administering one of the best systems devised in the world and that India is making steady though slow progress. They do not know that a subtle but effective system of terrorism and an organized display of force, on the one hand, and the deprivation of all powers of retaliation or self-defense, on the other, have emasculated the people and induced in them the habit of simulation. This awful habit has added to the ignorance and the self-deception of the administrators. Section 124-A, under which I am happily charged, is perhaps the prince among the political sections of the Indian Penal Code designed to suppress the liberty of the citizen. Affection cannot be manufactured or regulated by law. If one has an affection for a person or system, one should be free to give the fullest expression to his disaffection, so long as he does not contemplate, promote, or incite to violence. But the section under which . . . I [am] charged is one under which mere promotion of disaffection is a crime. I have studied some of the cases tried under it, and I know that some of the most loved of India's patriots have been convicted under it. I consider it a privilege, therefore, to be charged under that section. I have endeavored to give in their briefest outline the reasons for my disaffection. I have no personal ill will against any single administrator, much less can I have any disaffection toward the king's person. But I hold it to be a virtue to be disaffected toward a government which in its totality has done more harm to India than any previous system. India is less manly under the British rule than she ever was before. Holding such a belief, I consider it to be a sin to have affection for the system. And it has been a precious privilege for me to be able to write what I have in the various articles, tendered in evidence against me.

The Importance of Non-Cooperation

In fact, I believe that I have rendered a service to India and England by showing in non-cooperation the way out of the unnatural state in which both are living. In my humble opinion, non-cooperation with evil is as much a duty as is cooperation with good. But in the past, non-cooperation has been deliberately expressed in violence to the evildoer. I am endeavoring to show to my countrymen that violent non-cooperation only multiplies evil and that as evil can only be sustained by violence, withdrawal of support of evil requires complete abstention from violence. Nonviolence implies voluntary submission to the penalty for non-cooperation with evil. I am here, therefore, to invite and submit cheerfully to the highest penalty that can be inflicted upon me for what in law is a deliberate crime and what appears to me to be the highest duty of a citizen. The only course open to you, the judge, is either to resign your post, and thus dissociate yourself from evil if you feel that the law you are called upon to administer is an evil and that in reality I am innocent, or to inflict on me the severest penalty if you believe that the system and the law you are assisting to administer are good for the people of this country and that my activity is therefore injurious to the public weal.

Human Rights, Democracy, and Women's Emancipation

Daw Aung San Suu Kyi

Born in Rangoon, Burma, Daw Aung San Suu Kyi, the daughter of General Aung San and Daw Khin Kyi, spent her teenage and early adult years in India, Britain, and the United States. In 1947, her father, known as the founder of independent Burma and widely revered, was assassinated. In 1988 millions of Burmese citizens demonstrated for democracy by protesting the twenty-six year rule of the Burma Socialist Programme Party. The military responded by killing thousands of people. During that time, San Suu Kyi returned to Burma and addressed a rally of a half-million people in Rangoon, calling for a democratic government.

Inspired by the nonviolent campaigns of the American civil rights leader Martin Luther King Jr. and India's Mahatma Gandhi, San Suu Kyi organized more rallies and traveled throughout the country calling for peaceful democratic reforms and open elections. She gained national recognition as one of the leaders of the National League for Democracy (NLD), a political party that opposes the military government currently in power. Many of the NLD's leaders and party members have been sent to forced labor camps and prisons. In 1989, due to her alleged attempt to split the army (a charge that she denies), San Suu Kyi was detained by Myanmar's State Law

From a speech delivered by Daw Aung San Suu Kyi on videotape to the Non-Governmental Organization Forum on Women, in Huairou, China, August 31, 1995.

and Order Restoration Council (SLORC) for endangering the state's safety.

The NLD grew and went on to win by an over-whelming majority (82 percent) in national elections in 1990. The military regime, however, refused to relinquish power and stepped up repression of the NLD by renewed efforts to imprison and sometimes murder its members.

Like the South African leader Nelson Mandela, San Suu Kyi has come to be seen internationally as a symbol of heroic and peaceful resistance in the face of oppres-sion. She was awarded the Nobel Prize for Peace in 1991, by which time she had been under house arrest for two of what was to become six years.

Despite San Suu Kyi's official release from house ar-rest, there are still *de facto* restrictions on her freedom to move and speak, and oppression of pro-democracy ac-tivism continues. Burma's (Myanmar's) human rights record has been rated as one of the worst in the world, second only to Algeria.

San Suu Kyi gave the following opening keynote speech via videotape to the Non-Government Organiza-tion's (NGO) Forum on Women held in Huairou, China, in 1995. She gave the speech in absentia due to fears that she would not be allowed to return to her country if she attended the conference. The NGO Forum on Women was held in conjunction with the United Nation's Confer-ence on Women in Beijing, an event that attracted hun-dreds of thousands of women from around the world.

There was a great deal of disagreement and contro-versy around who would attend the event, especially in the United States. First Lady Hillary Clinton and Secre-tary of State Madeleine Albright were both invited to give keynote addresses at the event. However, questions were raised about whether it was appropriate for such visible political figures to give speeches in a country known for its human rights abuses. Finally it was decided that the White House would loosen its policies for this landmark international event. Even greater controversy was caused by China's decision not to allow the NGO part of the conference to take place in Beijing where the UN conference was being held. The NGO conference included many organizations that had been strong critics of China's human rights record. By locating the two conferences in two different cities, China was able to split the media attention and hence deflate the effect of controversial statements made against China. While China accomplished its objective of deflecting potential negative media attention and critics, it was also able to limit the size of the NGO conference venues. They did not accommodate the numbers of people who wanted to attend. A perfect case in point was the movie theater where the screening of San Suu Kyi's keynote address was given. The movie theater held 1,500, while a reported 4,500 people attempted to attend; 3,000 were turned away. This certainly was a consistent pattern of curtailing exposure to San Suu Kyi's message.

In the following speech, San Suu Kyi covers a range of human rights issues: a people's struggle for self-determination as a nation as well as tolerance and respect for women and the lives of their children. She outlines the need for peace, tolerance, and security in the lives of all peoples while focusing on the contributions and struggles of women throughout the world. San Suu Kyi contends that increasing women's involvement in politics and government will lead to increased social justice and peace worldwide.

It is a wonderful but daunting task that has fallen on me to say a few words by way of opening this Forum, the greatest concourse of women—joined by a few brave men—that has ever gathered on our planet. I want to try and voice some of the common hopes which firmly unite us in our splendid diversity.

But first I would like to explain why I cannot be with you in person today. Last month I was released from almost six years of house arrest. The regaining of my freedom has in turn imposed a duty on me to work for the freedom of women and men in my country who have suffered far more—and who continue to suffer far more—than I have. It is this duty which prevents me from joining you today. Even sending this message to you has not been without difficulties. . . .

The convener of this forum suggested that among [the] global forces and challenges [affecting the quality of life of the human community], I might wish to concentrate on those matters which occupy all my waking thoughts these days: peace, security, human rights and democracy. I would like to discuss these issues particularly in the context of the participation of women in politics and governance.

For millennia women have dedicated themselves almost exclusively to the task of nurturing, protecting and caring for the young and the old, striving for conditions of peace that favor life as a whole. To this can be added the fact that, to the best of my knowledge, no war was ever started by women. But it is women and children who have always suffered most in situations of conflict. Now that we are gaining control of the primary historical role imposed on us of sustaining life in the context of the home and family, it is time to apply in the arena of the world the wisdom and experience thus gained in activities of peace over so many thousands of years. The education and empowerment of women throughout the world cannot fail to result in a more caring, tolerant, just and peaceful life for all.

If to these universal benefits of the growing emancipation of women can be added the "peace dividend" for human development offered by the end of the Cold War, spending less on the war toys of grown men and much more on the urgent needs of humanity as a whole, then truly the next millennia will be an age the like of which has never been seen in human history. But there still remain many obstacles to be overcome before we can achieve this goal. And not least among those obstacles are intolerance and insecurity.

Tolerance vs. Insecurity

This year is the International Year for Tolerance. The United Nations has recognized that "tolerance, human rights, democracy and peace are closely related. Without tolerance, the foundations that form democracy and respect for human rights cannot be strengthened, and the achievement of peace will remain elusive." My own experience during the years I have been engaged in the democracy movement of Burma has convinced me of the need to emphasize the positive aspect of tolerance. It is not enough simply to "live and let live": genuine tolerance requires an active effort to try to understand the point of view of others; it implies broad-mindedness and vision, as well as confidence in one's own ability to meet new challenges without resorting to intransigence or violence. In societies where men are truly confident, women are not merely tolerated, they are valued. Their opinions are listened to with respect; they are given their rightful place in shaping the society in which they live.

There is an outmoded Burmese proverb still recited by men who wish to deny that women too can play a part in bringing necessary change and progress to their society: "The dawn rises only when the rooster crows." But Burmese people today are well aware of the scientific reasons behind the rising of dawn and the falling of dusk. And the intelligent rooster surely realizes that it is because dawn comes that it crows and not the other way 'round. It crows to welcome the light that has come to relieve the darkness of night. It is not the prerogative of men alone to bring light to this world: women with their capacity for compassion and self-sacrifice, their courage and perseverance, have done much to dissipate the darkness of intolerance and hate, suffering and despair.

Often the other side of the coin of intolerance is insecurity. Insecure people tend to be intolerant, and their intolerance unleashes forces that threaten the security of others. And where there is no security there can be no lasting peace. In its "Human Development Report" for this year the UNDP [United Nations Development Programme] noted that human security "is not a concern with weapons—it is a concern with human life and dignity." The struggle for democracy and human rights in Burma is a struggle for life and dignity. It is a struggle that encompasses our political, social and economic aspirations. The people of my country want the two freedoms that spell security: freedom from want and freedom from fear. It is want that has driven so many of our young girls across our borders to a life of sexual slavery where they are subject to constant humiliation and ill-treatment. It is fear of persecution for their political beliefs that has made so many of our people feel that even in their own homes they cannot live in dignity and security.

The Need for Partnership and Trust

Traditionally the home is the domain of the woman. But there has never been a guarantee that she can live out her life there safe and unmolested. There are countless women who are subjected to severe cruelty within the heart of the family which should be their haven. And in times of crisis when their menfolk are unable to give them protection, women have to face the harsh challenges of the world outside while continuing to discharge their duties within the home.

Many of my male colleagues who have suffered imprisonment for their part in the democracy movement have spoken of the great debt of gratitude they owe to their womenfolk, particularly to their wives who stood by them firmly, tender as mothers nursing their newly born, brave as lionesses defending their young. These magnificent human beings who have done so much to aid their men in the struggle for peace and justice—how much more could they not achieve if given the opportunity to work in their own right for the good of their country and of the world?

Our endeavors have also been sustained by the activities of strong and principled women all over the world who have campaigned not only for my release but, more importantly, for our cause. I cannot let this opportunity pass without speaking of the gratitude we feel towards our sisters everywhere, from heads of government to busy housewives. Their efforts have been a triumphant demonstration of female solidarity and of the power of an ideal to cross all frontiers.

In my country at present, women have no participation in the higher levels of government and none whatsoever in the judiciary. Even within the democratic movement only fourteen out of the 485 MPs [members of Parliament] elected in 1990 were women—all from my own party, the National League for Democracy. These fourteen women represent less than three percent of the total number of successful candidates. They, like their male colleagues, have not been permitted to take office since the outcome of those elections has been totally ignored. Yet the very high performance of women in our educational system and in the management of commercial enterprises proves their enormous potential to contribute to the betterment of society in general. Meanwhile our women have yet to achieve those fundamental rights of free expression, association and security of life denied also to their menfolk.

The adversities that we have had to face together have taught all of us involved in the struggle to build a truly democratic political system in Burma that there are no gender barriers that cannot be overcome. The relationship between men and women should, and can be, characterized not by patronizing behavior or exploitation, but by metta (that is to say loving kindness), partnership and trust. We need mutual respect and understanding between men and women, instead of patriarchal domination and degradation, which are expressions of violence and engender counter-violence. We can learn from each other and help one another to moderate the "gender weaknesses" imposed on us by traditional or biological factors.

People Must Participate Fully

There is an age-old prejudice the world over to the effect that women talk too much. But is this really a weakness? Could it not in fact be a strength? Recent scientific research on the human brain has revealed that women are better at verbal skills while men tend towards physical action. Psychological research has shown on the other hand that disinformation engendered by men has a far more damaging effect on its victims than feminine gossip. Surely these discoveries indicate that women have a most valuable contribution to make in situations of conflict, by leading the way to solutions based on dialogue rather than on viciousness and violence.

The Buddhist *Pavarana* ceremony at the end of the rainy season retreat was instituted by the Lord Buddha, who did not want human beings to live in silence, I quote, "like dumb animals." This ceremony, during which monks ask mutual forgiveness for any offense given during the retreat, can be said to be a council of truth and reconciliation. It might also be considered a forerunner of that most democratic of institutions, the parliament, a meeting of peoples gathered together to talk over their shared problems. All the world's great religions are dedicated to the generation of happiness and harmony. This demonstrates the fact that together with the combative instincts of man there exists a spiritual aspiration for mutual understanding and peace.

This forum of non-governmental organizations represents the belief in the ability of intelligent human beings to resolve conflicting interests through exchange and dialogue. It also represents the conviction that governments alone cannot resolve all the problems of their countries. The watchfulness and active cooperation of organizations outside the spheres of officialdom are necessary to ensure the four essential components of the human development paradigm as identified by the UNDP: productivity, equity, sustainability and empowerment. The last is particularly relevant: it requires that "development must be by people, not only for them. People must participate fully in the decisions and processes that shape their lives." In other words people must be allowed to play a significant role in the governance of their country. And "people" include women, who make up at least half the population of the world.

The last six years afforded me much time and food for thought. I came to the conclusion that the human race is not divided into two opposing camps of good and evil. It is made up of those who are capable of learning and those who are incapable of doing so. Here I am not talking of learning in the narrow sense of acquiring an academic education, but of learning as the process of absorbing those lessons of life that enable us to increase peace and happiness in out world. Women in their role as mothers have traditionally assumed the responsibility of teaching children values that will guide them throughout their lives. It is time we were given the full opportunity to use our natural teaching skills to contribute towards building a modern world that can withstand the tremendous challenges of the technological revolution which has in turn brought revolutionary changes in social values.

As we strive to teach others, we must have the humility to acknowledge that we too still have much to learn. And we must have the flexibility to adapt to the changing needs of the world around us. Women who have been taught that modesty and pliancy are among the prized virtues of our gender are marvelously equipped for the learning process. But they must be given the opportunity to turn these often merely passive virtues into positive assets for the society in which they live.

These, then, are our common hopes that unite us—that as the shackles of prejudice and intolerance fall from our own limbs we can together strive to identify and remove the impediments to human development everywhere. The mechanisms by which this great task is to be achieved provide the proper focus of this forum. I feel sure that women throughout the world who, like me, cannot be with you join me now in sending you all our prayers and good wishes for a joyful and productive meeting.

I thank you.

CHAPTER
TWO

The Right to Free Speech and Worship

"We Also Have a Religion"

Chief Red Jacket

Red Jacket, whose name was inspired by the British military coat he wore, was the last powerful chief of the Seneca tribe and a prominent figure of the Iroquois confederation, a coalition of six Indian tribes whose territory spanned present-day New York State and a large part of southeastern Ontario. Red Jacket thought of himself as an orator, rather than as a warrior. He was originally an ally of the British but eventually sought peace with the United States and influenced his people to support the United States against Britain in the War of 1812. He was a strong advocate for indigenous rights and encouraged his fellow Iroquois to preserve their own beliefs and traditions. He spoke out repeatedly at councils, treaty sessions, and before U.S. government officials for the right of Indians to lead their own lives in peace.

Red Jacket gave the following speech near Buffalo, New York, after a Boston missionary, Reverend Cram, in an effort to convert and baptize a tribe of Indians, delivered a sermon about the one "true" way to worship. Red Jacket stood up and spoke out for the tribe's right to free worship.

Friend and Brother! It was the will of the Great Spirit that we should meet together this day. He orders all things, and he has given us a fine day for our council. He has taken his garment from before the sun and has caused

---

From a speech by Sagoyewatha, aka "Red Jacket," to Christian missionaries who tried to convert his tribe, near Buffalo, New York, 1805.

the bright orb to shine with brightness upon us. Our eyes are opened so that we see clearly. Our ears are unstopped so that we have been able to distinctly hear the words which you have spoken. For all these favors we thank the Great Spirit and him only.

Brother! This council fire was kindled by you. It was at your request that we came together at this time. We have listened with attention to what you have said. You have requested us to speak our minds freely. This gives us great joy, for we now consider that we stand upright before you, and can speak what we think. All have heard your voice and all speak to you as one man. Our minds are agreed.

Brother! You say that you want an answer to your talk before you leave this place. It is right that you should have one, as you are a great distance from home, and we do not wish to detain you. But we will first look back a little, and tell you what our fathers have told us, and what we have heard from the white people.

Our Fathers Owned This Great Island

Brother! Listen to what we say. There was a time when our forefathers owned this great island [meaning the continent of North America—a common belief among the Indians]. Their seats extended from the rising to the setting of the sun. The Great Spirit had made it for the use of Indians. He had created the buffalo, the deer, and other animals for food. He made the bear and the deer, and their skins served us for clothing. He had scattered them over the country, and had taught us how to take them. He had caused the earth to produce corn for bread. All this he had done for his red children because he loved them. If we had any disputes about hunting grounds, they were generally settled without the shedding of much blood. But an evil day came upon us. Your forefathers crossed the great waters and landed on this island. Their numbers were small. They found friends and not enemies. They told us they had fled from their own country for fear of wicked men, and had come here to enjoy their religion. They asked for a small seat. We took pity on them, granted their request and they sat down amongst us. We gave them corn and meat. They gave us poison [alcohol] in return. The white people had now found our country. Tidings were carried back and more came amongst us. Yet we did not fear them. We took them to be friends. They called us brothers. We believed them and gave them a large seat. At length their numbers had greatly increased. They wanted more land. They wanted our country. Our eyes were opened, and our minds became uneasy. Wars took place. Indians were hired to fight against Indians, and many of our people were destroyed. They also brought strong liquors among us. It was strong and powerful and has slain thousands.

Brother! Our seats were once large, and yours were very small. You have now become a great people, and we have scarcely a place left to spread our blankets. You have got our country, but you are not satisfied. You want to force your religion upon us.

Brother! Continue to listen. You say that you are sent to instruct us how to worship the Great Spirit agreeably to his mind; and if we do not take hold of the religion which you white people teach we shall be unhappy hereafter. You say that you are right, and we are lost. How do you know this to be true? We understand that your religion is written in a book. If it was intended for us as well as for you, why has not the Great Spirit given it to us; and not only to us, but why did he not give to our forefathers the knowledge of that book, with the means of understanding it rightly? We only know what you tell us about it. How shall we know when to believe, being so often deceived by the white people?

We Do Not Wish to Destroy Your Religion

Brother! You say there is but one way to worship and serve the Great Spirit. If there is but one religion, why do you white people differ so much about it? Why not all agree, as you can all read the book?

Brother! We do not understand these things. We are told that your religion was given to your forefathers and has been handed down, father to son. We also have a religion which was given to our forefathers, and has been handed down to us, their children. We worship that way. It teaches us to be thankful for all the favors we received, to love each other, and to be united. We never quarrel about religion.

Brother! The Great Spirit has made us all. But he has made a great difference between his white and red children. He has given us a different complexion and different customs. To you he has given the arts; to these he has not opened our eyes. We know these things to be true. Since he has made so great a difference between us in other things, why may not we conclude that he has given us a different religion, according to our understanding? The Great Spirit does right. He knows what is best for his children. We are satisfied.

Brother! We do not wish to destroy your religion, or to take it from you. We only want to enjoy our own.

Brother! You say you have not come to get our land or our money, but to enlighten our minds. I will now tell you that I have been at your meetings and saw you collecting money from the meeting. I cannot tell what this money was intended for, but suppose it was for your minister; and if we should conform to your way of thinking, perhaps you may want some from us.

Brother! We are told that you have been preaching to the white people in this place. These people are our neighbors. We are acquainted with them. We will wait a little while, and see what effect your preaching has upon them. If we find it does them good and makes them honest and less disposed to cheat Indians, we will then consider again what you have said.

Brother! You have now heard our answer to your talk, and this is all we have to say at present. As we are going to part, we will come and take you by the hand, and hope the Great Spirit will protect you on your journey, and return you safe to your friends.

Free Speech Is a Fundamental Right

Jean-Paul Marat

Trained as a physician and scientist, Jean-Paul Marat was a central figure in the French Revolution. In 1789, Marat began to publish his own newspaper, *L'Ami du Peuple* (*The Friends of the People*). He wrote and spoke out about the inequities within society. Marat's oratorical skills gained him popularity among the lower classes. He incited the public to take direct action against social injustices imposed by the class-dominated political system and proposed social legislation that would accomplish those goals.

In 1792, Parisians elected Marat to be one of their representatives in the newly formed National Convention. During its first meeting in September 1792, members abolished the monarchy, set up the republic, and tried the king for treason. They also began to draw up a new constitution that guaranteed universal male suffrage, free public education, and subsidies to poor families. However, instead of forming a democracy, the Convention established a war dictatorship that operated through a number of committees, agencies, and tribunals. The two major political powers, the conservative Girondists and the leftist Jacobins wielded the greatest power during these years.

The Jacobins, formed in 1789, influenced the direction of the National Assembly through the public pressure they fueled by the effective use of their journals, like Marat's *The Friends of the People*. Originally the Jacobins included moderates and, for the most part, its membership belonged to the Parisian bourgeois. However, as the revo-

From Jean-Paul Marat's defense speech before the French Revolutionary Tribunal, Paris, 1793.

lution continued a small minority grew more radical and advocated for universal manhood suffrage. Marat belonged to that minority, along with Maximilien Robespierre and Georges Danton. In the National Convention, the Jacobins and other leftist opponents of the Girondists sat in raised seats and were called "the Mountain."

In contrast, the membership of the Girondists represented the educated, more provincial middle classes of the provinces. They worked as lawyers, journalists, and merchants, desired a constitutional government, and advocated for a continental war. In 1792 they succeeded in their early efforts by declaring war on Austria. The Girondists championed the provinces and attempted to prevent the trial of King Louis XVI and his eventual death sentence. They attacked the reputation of many of the Jacobins, specifically Marat.

Marat was disliked by many for his radical views. Not only were his political ideas extreme, his appearance was considered unkempt. This was not helped by the fact that he had a visible chronic skin disease. Marat began to focus his attacks on the Girondists. They rallied by arresting him under a law called the "Decree and Act of Accusation," for statements he made in an address to the Jacobins. In the following speech, Marat successfully defends himself by arguing that the address that was attributed to him as a crime had actually been signed by all "the Mountain" and would soon be signed "by all good citizens of France." In addition, he speaks of his right "to say, write, or do anything which accords with the sincere purpose of serving the country." Marat eloquently argues that the inalienable right to free speech is essential to the preservation of liberty. Marat's arguments not only freed him from imprisonment, they set the stage for the demise of the Girondists.

Due to the attacks made against Marat and others, the failure of the war they had so strongly supported, and their opposition to workers' demands for economic controls, public sentiment turned against Girondists. In May 1793, due to rising hostility against them, the Girondists were ousted from power.

In turn, three months after Marat gave this brilliant speech, he was murdered in his bathtub by Charlotte Corday, a conservative Girondin. Marat's martyrdom served his revolutionary cause as much as his actions did in life. While admired before his death, his popularity only grew stronger following his death.

Citizens, Members of the Revolutionary Tribunal: If [Jean Marie] Roland [de la Platière] the patron of the clique of the Girondists [political group of moderate republicans during the French Revolution] had not wasted the public property in misleading the people and perverting the public mind; if the faction of statesmen had not flooded the whole republic with infamous libels of the Commune, the municipality, the sections, the committee of surveillance, and, above all, directed against the deputation of Paris; if they had not so long laid their heads together to defame [Georges] Danton, [Maximilien] Robespierre, and Marat; if they had not ceaselessly represented me as a factionist, an anarchist, a drinker of blood, an ambitious man, who looked for supreme power under the title of tribune, triumvir, and director; if the nation, completely undeceived, had recognized the perfidy of these impostures; if their guilty authors had been branded, I would have resisted the arbitrary acts brought against me under the title of "Decree and Act of Accusation," by a perfidious faction, which I had so often denounced as almost wholly composed of royalists, traitors, and plotters. I would moreover have waited till the constitution had been reinforced by the return of patriotic deputies, before presenting myself at the tribunal, and thus have overwhelmed the vile wretches who are persecuting me today with such odious rancor.

If, therefore, I appear before my judges, it is only to rise triumphant and confound imposture; it is to unseal the eyes of that part of the nation which is already led astray on my account; it is to go out a conqueror from this imbroglio, to reassure public opinion, to do a good service to the fatherland, and to strengthen the cause of liberty.

Full of confidence in the enlightenment, the equity, and

the civic spirit of this tribunal, I myself urge the most rigorous examination of this affair. Strong in the testimony of my own conscience, in the rectitude of my intentions, in the purity of my civic spirit, I want no indulgence, but I demand strict justice.

I am ready to answer my judges. Nevertheless, before being examined I ought to place before you, citizens, a series of observations, which will put you in a position to judge of the crass ignorance, the absurdity, the iniquity, the perfidy, the implacableness, and the atrocity of my vile accusers.

False Accusations Violate Justice

The decree of accusation brought against me was carried without discussion, in violation of law and in contradiction of all the principles of order, liberty, and justice. For it is a principle of right that no citizen shall be censured without having first been heard. This decree of accusation was brought against me by two hundred and ten members of the faction of statesmen, contrary to the demand of ninety-two members of "the Mountain" [Jacobins]. That is to say, by two hundred and ten enemies of the country against ninety-two defenders of liberty. It was issued amid the most scandalous uproar, during which the patriots covered the royalists with opprobrium, reproaching them with their lack of civic spirit, their baseness, their machinations. It was issued in spite of the most marked manifestation of public opinion, amid the noise of continuous hootings throughout the tribunes. It was issued in a manner so revolting that twenty members who had been deceived by this faction of statemen refused to vote for it, the decree not having been discussed, and while one of them, yielding to the movement of an honest friend, cried out: "I do not vote, and I greatly fear, after all I have seen, that I have been the dupe of a perfidious cabal."

This decree, far from being the desire of the majority of the convention, as it is the work of a part of the members not making one-third of the assembly, can be regarded only as resulting from the implacable spirit of this faction of the statesmen. You will see that it is the outcome of a criminal plot, for it started after the reading of a certain address to the Jacobins which I had signed as president of the society. This patriotic address, however, was no longer to be attributed to me as a crime, when nearly all my colleagues of "the Mountain" hastened to the desk to sign it. The address was truly republican, and has just been signed by all sections of Paris, and will very soon be signed by all good citizens of France.

Leaving the denunciation of this address which suggested the call for the decree of accusation, the decree naturally came to naught; but it was revived with fury by our enemies when they saw me mount the tribune to renew the proposition to hale [King] Louis Philippe D'Orleans before the Revolutionary Tribunal, and to put a price on the heads of the rebellious and fugitive Capets [former monarchs]; a proposition which brought despair to the statesmen, forcing them to place a cord about their own necks if they adopted it, or to confess themselves the partisans of D'Orleans and the Capet rebels, the supporters of royalism, and the accomplices of [Charles] Dumouriez, if they rejected it. You know with what violence they opposed it. Such a decree, therefore, is only an act of tyranny. It calls for resistance against oppression; and it cannot fail to prove revolting to all good citizens when once it shall be as well known in the departments as it is in Paris.

I pass to the act of accusation. Originating with a committee of legislation almost entirely composed of my most mortal enemies, all members of the faction, it was drawn with such want of reflection that it bears on its face all the characteristics of dense ignorance, falsehood, madness, fury, and atrocity. That act, at a glance, may be seen to be filled with glaring inconsistency, or we should rather say with the spirit of contradiction to the "Decree of Accusation" of which it served as the basis; for it makes no mention of the address drawn up by the Jacobins, the signing of which they attributed to me as a crime; yet this address was what caused the Decree.

When I show how ridiculous and destitute of foundation this act is I feel ashamed of the committee. As the address of the Jacobins contains the sentiments of true republicans, and as it has been signed by nearly all of my colleagues of "the Mountain," the committee, forced to abandon the fundamental count in the accusation, was reduced to the expedient of citing some of my writings which had lain neglected for many months in the dust of their cases, and it stupidly reproduced the denunciation of some others of my writings, a subject which the assembly refused to pursue, passing to the order of the day, as I shall prove in the sequel.

Let us prove now that that act is illegal. It rests wholly, as you have seen, on some of my political opinions. These opinions had almost all been enunciated from the tribune of the convention before being published in my writings. For my writings, whose constant aim is to reveal plots, to unmask traitors, to propose useful measures, are a supplement to what I cannot always explain in the midst of the assembly. Now, article number seven of the fifth section of the "Constitutional Act" states in express terms:—

> The representatives of the nation are inviolable: they cannot be sought, accused, nor judged at any time for what they have said, written, or done in the exercise of their functions as representatives.

The "Act of Accusation" is, therefore, null and void, in that it is diametrically opposed to the fundamental law, which has not been and which cannot be repealed. It is null and void in that it attacks the most sacred right that belongs to a representative of the people.

The Right to Speak

I am quite aware that this right does not include that of plotting against the state, of attempting any enterprise against the interests of liberty, of attacking the rights of citizens, or of compromising public safety, but it certainly allows a citizen to say, write, or do anything which accords with the sincere purpose of serving the country, of procuring the general welfare, and causing the triumph of liberty. It is so essentially inherent in the functions of the nation's representatives that without it it would be impossible for the faithful to defend the fatherland and themselves against the traitors who would oppress and enslave them.

The patriots of the Constituent Assembly so thoroughly felt the necessity of making the representatives inviolable and unas-

sailable, capable of struggling with impunity against the despot
and completing the revolution, that they hastened to consecrate
this right by the famous decree of June 23, 1789, before they
had even constituted themselves the National Assembly.

They felt so thoroughly that this right was inherent in
every public function, that they stretched it to cover every judicial body, every administrative body, and even all citizens
united in a primary assembly.

Without this inalienable right could liberty maintain itself a moment against the machinations of its conspiring enemies? Without it, how, in the midst of a corrupt senate,
could a small number of deputies, invincibly attached to the
fatherland, unmask the traitors who seek to oppress it or put
it in fetters?

Without that essential right, how could a small number
of far-seeing and determined patriots foil the plots of a numerous faction of schemers? One may judge of this by what
happens to us. If the faction of statesmen can under false pre-
text attack me, expel me from its convention, hale me before
a tribunal, hold me in captivity, cause me to perish; tomorrow under other pretexts it will attack Robespierre, Danton,
Callot-d'Herbois, Panis, Lindet, Camille, David, Audoin,
Laiguelit, Meaulle, Dupuis, Javougues, Granet, and all the
other courageous deputies of the convention. It will restrain
the others by terror. It will usurp the sovereignty. It will call
to its side Dumouriez, Cobourg, Clerfayt, its accomplices.
Supported by Prussians, Austrians, and "Emigrants," it will
reestablish despotism in the hands of a Capet who will cut
the throats of all the known patriots, and it will endow the
first employments with the treasures of the state. The decree
of accusation issued against me for my political opinions is
therefore an attack on national representation, and I do not
doubt that the convention, with its quota filled by the return
of patriotic commissaries, will soon feel its dangerous consequences, its ill-boding results, and will blush that it should
have been decreed in its name, and will hasten to repeal it as
destructive of all public liberty.

The act of accusation is not only absurd in that it violates
all constitutional liberty and attacks national representa-
tions, it is still more so in that the committee, contrary to all

principle, turns the convention into a criminal tribunal, for it makes it pronounce without shame an iniquitous judgment, in deciding, without preliminary examination of a single document, without even having placed in question if such writings are mine, that I am found to have provoked murder and pillage, to have called up a power that threatens the sovereignty of the people, dishonored the convention, incited its dissolution, etc.

But what will appear incredible is that the committee calls down, without ceremony, without shame, and without remorse, capital punishment on my head, and cites articles of the penal code, which, according to it, condemned me to death. I doubt not that such is the object they have in view. How many statesmen have been tormented with despair of keeping me in prison, smothering my voice, and restraining my pen? Did not one of them, the atrocious Lacaze, have the impudence to ask the convention, as Dumouriez and Cobourg asked of the faction, that I should be outlawed? So that the act of accusation is a veritable "verdict rendered," which has only now to be executed.

Finally, this act is a tissue of lies and fabrications. It accuses me of having incited to murder and pillage, of setting up a "Chief of State," dishonoring and dissolving a convention, etc. The contrary was proved by the simple reading of my writings. I demand a consecutive reading of the denounced members; for it is not by garbling and mutilating passages that the ideas of an author are to be learnt, it is by reading the context that their meaning may be judged of.

If after the reading any doubts remain, I am here to remove them.

Citizens Must Have the Right to Criticize Their Leaders

Wei Jingsheng

Wei Jingsheng, born in 1950, gained prominence as a Chinese dissident during the late 1970s. Wei's parents were high ranking officials in the Communist Party and he was acquainted with Mao Zedong and his wife, Jiang Qing, at an early age. As a teenager he took part in the Cultural Revolution by serving in the Red Guard, a youth group considered by Mao to be his visionaries for the future of the Chinese Communist Party. Mao promoted the youthful and violent enthusiasm of the Red Guard to help reestablish his political power, to reinvigorate the country with revolutionary spirit, and to extinguish any remnants of opposition to the revolution. As a result, a great deal of violence took place, and tens of thousands of people were murdered. Mao had to then suppress the revolutionary fervor he had advocated by arresting many of those in the Red Guard. Wei was one of those people. He was arrested and imprisoned for several months in 1967. Upon his release he became involved in a publication called *Preparation*. However, fearing re-arrest, Wei fled to the remote countryside of China.

In the country, Wei gained new experiences that deepened his political education and awareness. He saw what life was like for those who lived outside the relative luxury and privileged urban environment of Beijing. He witnessed firsthand the poverty that resulted from Mao's agricultural modernization efforts. This education contin-

From Wei Jingsheng's defense speech at his trial in Beijing, China, October 1979.

ued when he served four years in an army comprised primarily of peasants. He began to pinpoint the blatant contradictions in the phrase "the people's democratic dictatorship." He addresses many of these apparent contradictions in the following speech.

Reflecting back upon this time in the 1960s and early 1970s, he began to realize that if the word "democracy" was to be used honestly, the political system must allow for the discussion of a diversity of opinions. He began to discover that this was impossible within the context of a dictatorship.

As a result of this political awakening, Wei began to write "wall posters"—posters that are written and then posted in visible places so that many people may read them. After Mao died in 1976, the youth of China began to demand greater freedoms. Their voices began to be heard and seen in an area near Tienanmen Square in Beijing called the "democracy wall." Wei wrote a poster called "Democracy: The Fifth Modernization" in response to the "Four Modernizations" outlined by Deng Xiaoping, the new leader of China. Deng's vision emphasized the need for China to modernize in science and technology, industry, agriculture, and the military. Wei commented on these propositions and advocated for the necessity of a fifth modernization, namely, democracy, before the other four could be accomplished. The content of his poster was also printed in *Exploration*, a magazine edited by Wei and his colleagues. Many were influenced by his ideas and began to see him as a leader in the democratic movement. As a result of the content of this poster and article, the government arrested Wei for engaging in counterrevolutionary activities.

In the following speech, delivered at his trial, Wei responds to the charges made against him. He states each charge and then proceeds to refute the reasoning behind the charge. In response to the first charge, that he revealed national secrets to the enemy, he asserts that he never knew any national secrets, but only rumors that all citizens in China discussed with openness. Most significantly, Wei asserts the right of Chinese citizens to criticize

rather than to deify their leaders. He insists on the right
to speak freely and the need for democratic changes
within China to ensure the economic modernizations advocated by Deng.

At the end of his trail, the judge convicted Wei to a
fourteen-year prison term that would include many years
spent in an isolation cell and in labor camps. Wei's imprisonment from 1979 until 1993 only served to
strengthen the democratic cause within China. He became a national hero to those involved in the democratic
movement. Eventually this movement led to massive
demonstrations in Tienanmen Square in 1989, which
were crushed by the Chinese army. In 1997, Wei traveled
to the United States to receive medical treatment for injuries incurred during his imprisonment. Since then he
has been living and teaching in the United States. As a
political exile he continues to fight for democracy and the
improvement of human rights in his native land.

I see as unfounded and unsubstantiated the charges in the
indictment brought by the People's Procuratorate of
Peking's Municipality. My editing of publications and my
writing of posters were both in accordance with Article 45 of
the constitution: "Citizens enjoy freedom of speech, corre-
spondence, the press, assembly, association, procession,
demonstration and the freedom to strike, and have the right
to 'speak out freely, air their views fully, hold great debates
and write big-character posters.'" Our reasons for producing
our publication were simply to attempt a tentative exploration of the path along which China could advance this objective. Our activities, motivated by the principles I have just
mentioned, are described as counterrevolutionary by the Public Security Department and the Procuratorate. We cannot accept such a description. I shall now go on to express substan-
tiated views on each of the charges listed in the indictment.

THE FIRST CHARGE. The indictment states that I provided foreigners with national military information and committed the crime of counterrevolution . . . the wording of the

new penal code and of the old Act for the Punishment of Counterrevolution reads alike: providing military information to *the enemy* constitutes the crime of treason. Yet, in the eyes of the Public Prosecutor, my discussions with English and French foreign correspondents are seen as treasonable conduct. Is this not as good as describing the English and French journalists as the enemy? I would like to draw the attention of the prosecution to the fact that when Hua Gofeng received the journalists of four Western European nations, he quite clearly addressed each correspondent from each nation as "my friend."

I Supplied the Enemy with Nothing at All

The constitution stipulates that it is the duty of all citizens to *keep national secrets*. Yet here, where the wording of the constitution is quite explicit on this aspect of the citizen's duties, the indictment uses the vague and hazy term *military intelligence*. It is common knowledge that a lot of what passes for military intelligence or information is obtainable by an analysis of what is stated in the public media of any nation's newspapers, radio and television news reports, etc. It is clear then that the term military information or intelligence is an over-generalized concept. Since it is the duty of all citizens to keep national secrets, this presupposes that the citizens know in the first place what the secrets are that they are supposed to keep. That is to say, this secret must be recognizable from the outset as a piece of classified information. It must be clearly indicated or marked down as a national or military secret. Only then do the citizens have the duty to maintain its secrecy. Never once in the period that followed the outbreak of the Sino-Vietnamese War did I come into contact with anything whatsoever marked as a classified secret. Thus, there is no question of my furnishing anyone with anything that can be described as secret by the terms of the legal definition. When I chatted with reporters and foreign diplomats from friendly nations it was difficult for me not to mention every aspect of the internal situation in our country. . . .

JUDGE: Talk slower, Wei Jingsheng.

WEI: Whether or not the news I mentioned in my conversations with foreigners was news which the government preferred not to divulge I had no means of knowing. Since I am just an ordinary citizen, my sources of information remain the grapevine and rumor, not official documents from a government source. Whether or not my information might have happened to coincide quite fortuitously with points of information marked as classified secrets in government documents I likewise have no means of telling, because I have never set eyes on any classified documents. But the news I discussed could not have had any harmful effect on the front-line situation. That was something to which I gave some thought before I said anything. In the instance of my mention of the name of the Commander-in-Chief at the front, whoever has heard of a victory being won because the Commander-in-Chief's name was not revealed? Conversely, whoever has heard of defeat being suffered simply because the enemy knew the name of one's own Commander-in-Chief? No cases of either kind exist, so in what way can my mention of his name have had an adverse effect on the front-line situation? Throughout the whole gamut of ancient and modern history, I have never heard of knowledge of the Commander-in-Chief's name proving to be a vital factor in the final outcome of hostilities. Such a theory just doesn't hold water.

Naturally, the public prosecutor may state that, according to established custom and practice in our nation, anything that comes into the authorities' heads may be considered a national secret. At the time when the "Gang of Four" [Jiang Qing, Mao's wife; Yao Wenyuan; Wang Bonowen; Zhang Chungiao. Jiang Qing and her three allies led an attack on traditional Chinese culture during the Cultural Revolution and Jiang attempted to succeed as leader of China after Mao's death. She failed and was imprisoned.] was in power, when the isolationist policy held sway and the nation was sealed off from the outside world behind closed doors, anything that appealed to the authorities became a national secret, and just to say a few words to a foreigner could, if the powers wished, be construed as having illicit relations with a foreign country. Perhaps the public prosecutor wants all citizens to abide by the established practices of the "Gang of Four" era? Or does

he just want them to adhere to the law? In this respect the Department of Public Security has already spoken, when it said
I must abide by the rules and regulations governing the main-
tenance of official secrets. I do not know what these rules and
regulations are. I do know that in themselves they refer to
keeping things secret; but, because they are not publicly pro-
mulgated for ordinary citizens to abide by, they can only be
something laid down by some internal bureau. The ordinary
citizen, therefore, may be obliged to abide by the constitution
and the law, but he is under no obligation to abide by rules
and regulations about which he knows nothing, since they
were made by some internal bureau.

To sum up. Firstly, I had no intention of betraying the fatherland. Secondly, I supplied the enemy with nothing at all.
Thirdly, I gave my friends no official secrets—either national
or military. Thus the prosecution's accusation that I committed treason is quite unfounded. If the prosecution considers
the content of my discussions with foreigners as things the
government would rather I had not mentioned, and that I
made a mistake by so doing, I am perfectly willing to accept
that. Moreover, I am perfectly willing to accept that, in response to the government's reasonable demands hereafter, it
is the duty of every citizen to maintain secrecy about matters
the government feels should be kept secret. But, in turn, I
trust the government will be able to be more explicit in its
stipulation of the actual scope of those secrets it expects its
citizens to maintain, and not leave them in a state of per-
plexed bewilderment; nor will it directly prevent Chinese nationals from having friendly relations with the nationals of
other countries, since all this will only further confuse the administration of justice and have adverse effects upon the nation and its people.

The Democratic Trend Is This Age's Revolutionary Current

THE SECOND CHARGE. The indictment states that I carried out counterrevolutionary propaganda and agitation, and
describes my essays, "Democracy: The Fifth Modernization," etc., as reactionary articles. Likewise our publication

Exploration is referred to as reactionary. In view of this, we must first make it clear what is meant by such terms as "reactionary," "counterrevolutionary" and "revolutionary."

As a result of the influence of all those years of cultural autocracy, and the obscurantist policy of keeping the people in a state of blind ignorance in the "Gang of Four" era, there are even now people whose outlook is that if one does things exactly in accordance with the will of the leadership currently in power, this is what is meant by being "revolutionary" whereas to run counter to the will of those currently in power is counterrevolutionary. I cannot agree with such a vulgar debasement of the concept of revolution. The term "revolutionary" entails following a course of action whereby one moves with the current of historical development, and strives to remove all that is old and conservative blocking and impeding the onward flow of history. Revolution is the struggle of new phenomena against old phenomena. To attach the label of perpetual revolution to the will and ambition of those currently in power is tantamount to stifling all diversity of thought; "Power is Truth." Such a vulgarization of the concept of revolution served as one of the most effective tools with which the "Gang of Four" suppressed anything remotely revolutionary and crushed the people into the ground for more than twenty years.

Now allow me to turn to the term "counterrevolutionary," and its valid and proper frame of reference. Strictly speaking, the term implies a historical approach to the examination of the political concept to be applied to a given problem. In the realm of politics there is no immutable concept, and at different historical periods, because the revolutionary trends or currents are different, each conception of the word counterrevolutionary differs, as indeed do the phenomena to which the term is applied. If one particular conception of the term (valid for one particular period) is made the norm, the result can only be the arbitrary attaching of labels to the wrong people. Even in times of revolution itself, because of the limits of the levels of understanding among the populace, there arise a number of conflicting interpretations of this one word counterrevolutionary. To use this term as an immutable political concept for assessing the guilt of those charged with crimes is like using the willow catkins floating in the breeze as a device for assessing altitude. This is the reason behind the great number of injustices, wrongs and misjudged cases which have arisen in this country over the past 30 years. It is also one of the reasons why the "Gang of Four" were able to gain power in the very teeth of popular resentment. The inevitable result of making the current political concept the legal norm or standard is an open invitation to be taken in and deceived by such terms as counter-revolutionary.

Next we come to the connection between my articles and the present revolutionary trend. The present historical trend or current is a democratic one. At this stage in the development of Chinese society, her population is confronted with the following problem: Unless there is a reform of the social system, accompanied by the eradication of the social origins of the dictatorial fascist autocracy, together with a thorough implementation of democracy and a guarantee of the people's democratic rights, then Chinese society will be unable to advance and the socialist modernization of the country be incapable of achievement. Thus, the democratic trend is this age's revolutionary current, while those autocratic conservatives who stand in opposition to the democratic trend are the real counterrevolutionaries of the age.

The central argument of those articles of mine, such as "Democracy: The Fifth Modernization," is that without democracy there will be no Four Modernizations; without the *fifth* modernization, or democracy, any talk of modernization will remain an empty lie. How does such an argument constitute counterrevolution? Surely it is those very people who oppose democracy who should be included in the counterrevolutionary category? Naturally I do not claim that the grounds of my argument and its thesis are always perfectly correct. They too must await the ultimate test of historical practice. They too must undergo all manner of criticism from every quarter, for only then can they be made more accurate. But even if the grounds of my argument and the underlying thesis are not completely accurate, this in no way impairs the revolutionary nature of my topic, which is clear in its argument.

Why Can't We Treat Marxism Critically?

THE THIRD CHARGE. The indictment states I slandered Marxism-Leninism and Mao Zedong Thought by likening it to an even more brilliant piece of quackery than any of the old itinerant pox-doctors' panaceas and poultices. My understanding of the term slander is that it refers to a person being groundlessly charged with a crime he has not committed. The manufacture of poultices and panaceas is no crime. By quoting me out of context and giving a garbled version of what I said, the prosecutor can hardly be said to have made out a case for slander.

The Marxism I attacked in my essays is in no way the Marxism of more than a hundred or so years ago, but rather the form of Marxism favored by that school of political con men such as Lin Biao and the "Gang of Four." I recognize nothing in this world as constantly immutable, nor any theory as absolutely correct. All ideological theory is relative, for within its existing context it contains elements of relative truth and, conversely, elements of relative absurdity. At one given time and in one given situation it may be a relatively accurate theory, whereas at another given time and situation it can be relatively preposterous. In the face of certain data it may be a correct theory, while in the face of different data it may appear absurd. Certain theories in themselves share at one and the same time the possibility of being correct and the possibility of being absurd. Marxism is in no way an exception. Marxism, over a hundred years of development, has been successively transformed into a number of divergent schools—Kautskyism, Leninism, Trotskyism, Stalinism, Mao Zedong Thought, Eurocommunism, etc. While these different theories all abide by the basic tenets of Marxism, or do so in part, they have also carried out partial modifications and revisions of Marxism as a system. Thus, though they are called Marxist, none of them is the original Marxist system. To a considerable extent the theoretical core of original Marxism is in part centered around a description of a proper society, an idealistic state which is by no means unique in its conception to Marxism alone. For such a society was a widespread aspiration, shared by the working classes and intellectuals alike in their hope for liberty and equality, public ownership of property, and social justice. The method Marxism advocated for the achievement of this ideal society was the fusing of common democracy with a dictatorship in which power had been centralized. It is this fusion which is the most striking characteristic of the Marxist tenets.

Following a hundred years of actual practice, those governments which have emerged from this method of dictatorship, where power has been concentrated—such as those of the Soviet Union, Vietnam, and China before smashing of the "Gang of Four"—have without exception deteriorated into fascist regimes, where a small leading faction imposes its autocracy over the large mass of ordinary laboring people. Moreover, the fascist dictators, in whose grasp the government has come to rest, have long since ceased to use the dictatorship of the proletariat as a tool of implementing the old ideals of Communism itself. Precisely the opposite is the case. For without exception these rulers have used the ideals of Communism to reinforce the so-called dictatorship of the proletariat so that it may function as a tool for the benefit of those in power.

Thus, Marxism's fate is common to that of several religions. After the second or third generation of transmission, its revolutionary substance is quietly removed, while its doctrinal ideals are partially taken over by the rulers, to be used as an excuse to enslave the people and as a tool to deceive and fool them. By this stage, the nature of its teachings has also undergone a basic change, in that the ideals become, respectively, the excuse and tool of enslavement and deception. Thus, the nature of the teachings has been fundamentally changed. I call the practice of using ideals to mislead and enslave people "idealism." (Others think of it as a matter of faith.) The feudal fascist dictatorship of the "Gang of Four" represented the culmination of such a development. When these forms of fascism make use of fine and glorious ideals to set up a blind faith in some modern superstition, so that the people may be the easier cheated and deceived, is this not a modern form of charlatanism? Is it not an even more brilliant panacea or poultice than those of the old nostrum-mongering pox-doctors?

Here I should point out that it was by basing my studies on the course of the historical development of Marxism that I reached these conclusions, and that any possible inaccuracies can be resolved by further theoretical inquiry. Though I welcome anyone's criticism of these conclusions of mine, regardless of their accuracy, according to the principle of the freedoms of discussion and publication, it does not constitute a crime to promote tentative theoretical inquiry and exchange such ideological conclusions with others. We should always adopt a critical approach to past ideological theory that still survives in actuality in the present age, and since this is the Marxist approach to pursuing studies, why can't we treat Marxism critically as well? Those who forbid the critical treatment of Marxism are engaged in the very process of transforming Marxism into a religious faith. Any man has the right to believe and adhere to the theories he holds to be correct, but he should not use legally binding stipulations to impose on others the theories he has faith in, otherwise he is interfering with the liberties of his fellow men.

Free Speech Is a Right

THE FOURTH CHARGE. The indictment claims that, by flaunting the banner of so-called free speech for democracy and human rights, I incited the overthrow of the socialist system and the political power of the dictatorship of the proletariat. First of all, allow me to point out there is nothing whatsoever "so-called" about free speech. On the contrary, it is stipulated by the constitution as a right to be enjoyed by all citizens. The Public Prosecutor's choice of such a term in discussing rights granted citizens by the constitution not only shows his prejudice when thinking on such matters, but further illustrates that he has forgotten his responsibility to protect the rights of his fellow citizens. He makes the rights of the citizens in this country of ours the object of ridicule.

I feel there is no need for me to refute item by item the public prosecutor's method of quoting me out of context when he is listing the charges against me. I would merely like to point out his carelessness and his negligence. In the indictment there appear the following words: "a system of feudal monarchism in the guise of socialism." Was not the "Gang of Four's" fascist dictatorship simply feudal monarchism in the guise of socialism? Again there appears this expression of mine, "nor serve as tools for the modernization of the ambitious aggrandizement by the dictatorship," which was followed in my original by, "we want the modernization of the people's lives." Don't tell me the prosecutor wants the modernization of ambitious aggrandizement by the dictatorship but does not want a real modernization of the people's lives? I don't think the prosecutor can be like that. I am also unwilling to believe that the prosecutor will forbid criticism of the "Gang of Four's" feudal fascism. Yet why then did I quote in evidence those illustrations? I do not desire to make improper comments. I merely know that those remarks of the prosecutor are in no way able to illustrate that I wanted to overthrow the government and the socialist system, nor are they able to illustrate that I was harming the democratic cause.

In the cause of the publication of our magazine *Exploration*, we never once joined up with any conspiratorial organization, nor did we ever take part in the activities of any violent organization. *Exploration* was on sale to the public as a publication designed to explore and probe theoretical problems; never did it make the overthrow of political power its aim, nor could it ever have been engaged in activities aimed at overthrow of the government. It saw itself as a part of the democratic cause, nor could it ever have harmed that cause. When people ask us if we were ever prepared to participate in armed struggle, or carry out actions aimed at the overthrow of the government, I have already supplied them a precise answer to such a question. I recognize legitimate propaganda and the democratic movement as the indispensable means to foster democratic government. Only when it has been understood by the majority will democratic government gradually come into being, through the reform of the old political system. This viewpoint was one of the basic aims of our publication. Yang Guang, Lu Lin, Zhao Nan, and Hu Qing can all bear witness to this fact. They have all heard what I have to say on this subject.

The public prosecutor's accusation that I wanted to overthrow the socialist system is even more at odds with the facts.

The prosecutor claims to have examined my essays, so he should have noticed that section within the article, "Democracy: The Fifth Modernization," called "Socialism and Democracy," which deals with my attitude toward socialism. On the many occasions that the prosecutor had talks with me, I also mentioned this same question, so he cannot say he does not know. Of course in the eyes of the prosecutor, his interpretation of a socialist system may possibly differ enormously from my conception of that system. I recognize that in reality the socialist system may take many different forms and not be one stereotype. In the light of their most obvious distinction, I would classify socialist systems into two large categories. The first is the Soviet-style of dictatorial socialism, with its chief characteristic of having its power concentrated in the hands of the minority in authority. The second category is democratic socialism, with the power reinvested in the whole people organized on a democratic footing. The majority of people in our nation all wish for the implementation of this kind of socialism. The aim of our exploratory inquiry was to seek the way to attain such a socialist system. My taking part in the democratic movement was with the aim of implementing this form of democratic socialism.

I consider that without carrying out a reform of the social system, without a true establishment of popular democratic power, and if there is no democratic system of government to act as a guarantee, then our nation's economic modernization cannot be attained. A democratic system of government is the prerequisite for our country's total modernization. This was the idea behind the title of my article "Democracy: The Fifth Modernization"; it was the central idea expounded in the same essay. Perhaps the members of the Office of the Procuratorate do not agree with my theory, but their disagreement with my theories does not brand me as someone wanting to overthrow the socialist system.

The Right to Criticize Leaders

THE FIFTH CHARGE. There is no need for me to refute item by item in the list of charges in the indictment those places where the prosecution quotes me out of context. I would only point out two things. First, the constitution grants citizens the right to criticize their leaders, because these leaders are not gods. It is only through the people's criticism and supervision that those leaders will make fewer mistakes, and only in this way that the people will avoid the misfortune of having their lords and masters ride roughshod over them. Then, and only then, will the people be able to breathe freely. Secondly, if we wish to carry out the reform of our nation's socialist system we must base this on the entire population using the methods of criticism and discussion to find out the defects in the present system; otherwise reforms cannot be successfully carried out. It is the people's prerogative, when faced by unreasonable people and unacceptable matters, to make criticisms. Indeed, it is also their unshirkable duty so to do and this is a sovereign right with which no individual or government organization has a right to interfere.

Criticism may not be beautiful or pleasant to hear, nor can it always be completely accurate. If one insists on criticism being pleasant to hear, and demands its absolute accuracy on pain of punishment, this is as good as forbidding criticism and banning reforms. In such a situation one might just as well deify the leadership outright. Surely we are not expected to retread that old path of blind faith in the leadership advocated by the "Gang of Four"? Naturally criticism should have substantial factual basis, nor should we tolerate personal attacks and malicious slandering. This taboo was one of the principles adhered to by our publication, as our introductory opening statement to our readers demonstrates. If the prosecution feels that in this respect I did not do enough, I am willing to accept the criticism put forward by the prosecution or anyone else.

That concludes my defense address. . . .

"We Are All Human Beings"

Tenzin Gyatso

Born in 1935, Tenzin Gyatso was identified as the Fourteenth Dalai Lama of Tibet at the age of four. He headed Tibet's theocracy until China invaded the country and annexed the area in 1950. A national uprising took place against the Chinese invasion in 1959. Forced to flee to India at that time, the Dalai Lama has lived in exile since then. Since 1959, China has systematically destroyed the Tibetan Buddhist culture. Monasteries were demolished and most Buddhist monks and nuns who did not escape to India were either murdered or sentenced to life imprisonment. In 1959 there were 200,000 monks and nuns living in Tibet. Today there are 1,000. Since 1989, the capital of Tibet, Lhasa, has been under Chinese martial law. It is illegal to fly the Tibetan flag, and in most schools students learn Chinese as their primary language rather than Tibetan. Ten thousand Chinese troops rule over the remaining 50,000 living Tibetans. Many of the international objections to China's human rights policy focus on the controversial treatment of the people and land of Tibet. The Dalai Lama considers himself to be a refugee.

The Dalai Lama was awarded the Nobel Prize in 1989. Since then, increased international attention has been paid to the status of Tibet and to the issue of human rights throughout the world, especially the rights of refugees forced into exile due to the actions of hostile governments.

The Dalai Lama gave the following speech in Oslo, Norway, when he received the Nobel Prize. In his speech,

From Tenzin Gyatso's, Fourteenth Dalai Lama of Tibet, Nobel Peace Prize acceptance speech, Oslo, Norway, December 10, 1989, as reprinted in *The Dalai Lama: A Policy of Kindness* (Ithaca, NY: Snow Lion Publications, 1990). Copyright © 1990 Sidney Piburn. Reprinted with permission from the publisher.

the Dalai Lama states that the "fundamental rights of the Tibetan peoples are still today being systematically violated." The Chinese have attempted to annihilate the Tibetan culture, its religious life, and its national customs, he contends. The Chinese government continues to marginalize the Tibetan people; ever increasing numbers of Chinese populate the country, threatening to reduce the Tibetans to a minority in their own country. In response to these developments, the Dalai Lama proposes several reforms, including "respect for the Tibetan people's fundamental human rights and democratic freedoms."

It is an honor and pleasure to be among you today. I am really happy to see so many old friends who have come from different corners of the world, and to make new friends, whom I hope to meet again in the future. When I meet people in different parts of the world, I am always reminded that we are all basically alike: we are all human beings. Maybe we have different clothes, our skin is of a different color, or we speak different languages. This is on the surface. But basically, we are the same human beings. That is what binds us to each other. That is what makes it possible for us to understand each other and to develop friendship and closeness.

Thinking over what I might say today, I decided to share with you some of my thoughts concerning the common problems all of us face as members of the human family. Because we all share this small planet earth, we have to learn to live in harmony and peace with each other and with nature. That is not just a dream, but a necessity. We are dependent on each other in so many ways that we can no longer live in isolated communities and ignore what is happening outside those communities. We need to help each other when we have difficulties, and we must share the good fortune that we enjoy. I speak to you as just another human being, as a simple monk. If you find what I say useful, then I hope you will try to practice it.

I also wish to share with you today my feelings concerning the plight and aspirations of the people of Tibet. The No-

bel Prize is a prize they well deserve for their courage and un-
failing determination during the past forty years of foreign
occupation. As a free spokesman for my captive countrymen
and -women, I feel it is my duty to speak out on their behalf.
I speak not with a feeling of anger or hatred towards those
who are responsible for the immense suffering of our people
and the destruction of our land, homes and culture. They too
are human beings who struggle to find happiness and deserve
our compassion. I speak to inform you of the sad situation in
my country today and of the aspirations of my people, because in our struggle for freedom, truth is the only weapon
we possess. . . .

Today We Are Truly a Global Family

Today, we are truly a global family. What happens in one
part of the world may affect us all. This, of course, is not
only true of the negative things that happen, but is equally
valid for the positive developments. We not only know what
happens elsewhere, thanks to the extraordinary modern
communications technology, we are also directly affected by
events that occur far away. We feel a sense of sadness when
children are starving in Eastern Africa. Similarly, we feel a
sense of joy when a family is reunited after decades of separation by the Berlin Wall. Our crops and livestock are conta-
minated and our health and livelihood threatened when a nuclear accident happens miles away in another country. Our
own security is enhanced when peace breaks out between
warring parties in other continents.

But war or peace; the destruction or the protection of nature; the violation or promotion of human rights and democratic freedoms; poverty or material well being; the lack of
moral and spiritual values or their existence and development; and the breakdown or development of human understanding, are not isolated phenomena that can be analyzed
and tackled independently of one another. In fact, they are
very much interrelated at all levels and need to be ap-
proached with that understanding. . . .

Peace can only last where human rights are respected,
where the people are fed, and where individuals and nations

are free. True peace with ourselves and with the world around us can only be achieved through the development of mental peace. The other phenomena mentioned above are similarly interrelated. Thus, for example, we see that a clean environment, wealth or democracy mean little in the face of war, especially nuclear war, and that material development is not sufficient to ensure human happiness.

The Importance of Inner Development

Material progress is of course important for human advancement. In Tibet, we paid much too little attention to technological and economic development, and today we realize that this was a mistake. At the same time, material development without spiritual development can also cause serious problems. In some countries too much attention is paid to external things and very little importance is given to inner development. I believe both are important and must be developed side by side so as to achieve a good balance between them. Tibetans are always described by foreign visitors as being a happy, jovial people. This is part of our national character, formed by cultural and religious values that stress the importance of mental peace through the generation of love and kindness to all other living sentient beings, both human and animal. Inner peace is the key: if you have inner peace, the external problems do not affect your deep sense of peace and tranquility. In that state of mind you can deal with situations with calmness and reason, while keeping your inner happiness. That is very important. Without this inner peace, no matter how comfortable your life is materially, you may still be worried, disturbed or unhappy because of circumstances.

Clearly, it is of great importance, therefore, to understand the interrelationship among these and other phenomena, and to approach and attempt to solve problems in a balanced way that takes these different aspects into consideration. Of course it is not easy. But it is of little benefit to try to solve one problem if doing so creates an equally serious new one. So really we have no alternative: we must develop a sense of universal responsibility not only in the geographic sense, but also in respect to the different issues that confront our planet.

Responsibility does not only lie with the leaders of our countries or with those who have been appointed or elected to do a particular job. It lies with each of us individually. Peace, for example, starts within each one of us. When we have inner peace, we can be at peace with those around us. When our community is in a state of peace, it can share that peace with neighboring communities, and so on. When we feel love and kindness towards others, it not only makes others feel loved and cared for, but it helps us also to develop inner happiness and peace. And there are ways in which we can consciously work to develop feelings of love and kindness. For some of us, the most effective way to do so is through religious practice. For others it may be non-religious practices. What is important is that we each make a sincere effort to take seriously our responsibility for each other and for the natural environment.

I am very encouraged by the developments which are taking place around us. After the young people of many countries, particularly in northern Europe, have repeatedly called for an end to the dangerous destruction of the environment which was being conducted in the name of economic development, the world's political leaders are now starting to take meaningful steps to address this problem. The report to the United Nations Secretary General by the World Commission on the Environment and Development (the Brundtland report) was an important step in educating governments on the urgency of the issue. Serious efforts to bring peace to war-torn zones and to implement the right to self-determination of some peoples have resulted in the withdrawal of Soviet troops from Afghanistan and the establishment of independent Namibia. Through persistent non-violent popular efforts dramatic changes, bringing many countries closer to real democracy, have occurred in many places, from Manila in the Philippines to Berlin in East Germany. . . .

Tibetan Exile

What these positive changes indicate is that reason, courage, determination, and the inextinguishable desire for freedom can ultimately win. In the struggle between forces of war, violence and oppression on the one hand, and peace, reason and freedom on the other, the latter are gaining the upper hand. This realization fills us Tibetans with hope that some day we too will once again be free.

The awarding of the Nobel Prize to me, a simple monk from far-away Tibet, here in Norway, also fills us Tibetans with hope. It means that, despite the fact that we have not drawn attention to our plight by means of violence, we have not been forgotten. It also means that the values we cherish, in particular our respect for all forms of life and the belief in the power of truth, are today recognized and encouraged. It is also a tribute to my mentor, Mahatma Gandhi, whose example is an inspiration to so many of us. . . .

As you know, Tibet has, for forty years, been under foreign occupation. Today, more than a quarter of a million Chinese troops are stationed in Tibet. Some sources estimate the occupation army to be twice this strength. During this time, Tibetans have been deprived of their most basic human rights, including the right to life, movement, speech, worship, only to mention a few. More than one sixth of Tibet's population of six million died as a direct result of the Chinese invasion and occupation. Even before the Cultural Revolution started, many of Tibet's monasteries, temples and historic buildings were destroyed. Almost everything that remained was destroyed during the Cultural Revolution. I do not wish to dwell on this point, which is well documented. What is important to realize, however, is that despite the limited freedom granted after 1979 to rebuild parts of some monasteries and other such tokens of liberalization, the fundamental human rights of the Tibetan people are still today being systematically violated. In recent months this bad situation has become even worse.

If it were not for our community in exile, so generously sheltered and supported by the government and people of India and helped by organizations and individuals from many parts of the world, our nation would today be little more than a shattered remnant of a people. Our culture, religion and national identity would have been effectively eliminated. As it is, we have built schools and monasteries in exile and have created democratic institutions to serve our people and preserve the seeds of our civilization. With this experience, we intend to implement full democracy in a future free Tibet. Thus, as we develop our community in exile on modern lines, we also cherish and preserve our own identity and culture and bring hope to millions of our countrymen and -women in Tibet.

The issue of most urgent concern at this time is the massive influx of Chinese settlers into Tibet. Although in the first decades of occupation a considerable number of Chinese were transferred into the eastern parts of Tibet—in the Tibetan provinces of Amdo (Chinghai) and Kham (most of which has been annexed by the neighboring Chinese province)—since 1983 an unprecedented number of Chinese have been encouraged by their government to migrate to all parts of Tibet, including central and western Tibet (which the PRC [People's Republic of China] refers to as the so-called Tibet Autonomous Region). Tibetans are rapidly being reduced to an insignificant minority in their own country. This development, which threatens the very survival of the Tibetan nation, its culture and spiritual heritage, can still be stopped and reversed. But this must be done now, before it is too late.

The new cycle of protest and violent repression, which started in Tibet in September of 1987 and culminated in the imposition of martial law in the capital, Lhasa, in March of this year, was in large part a reaction to this tremendous Chinese influx. Information reaching us in exile indicates that the protest marches and other peaceful forms of protest are continuing in Lhasa and a number of other places in Tibet despite the severe punishment and inhumane treatment given to Tibetans detained for expressing their grievances. The number of Tibetans killed by security forces during the protest in March and of those who died in detention afterwards is not known but is believed to be more than two hundred. Thousands have been detained or arrested and imprisoned, and torture is commonplace.

The Five Point Peace Plan

It was against the background of this worsening situation and in order to prevent further bloodshed, that I proposed what is generally referred to as the Five Point Peace Plan for the restoration of peace and human rights in Tibet. . . .

The Five Point Peace Plan addresses the principal and interrelated issues, which I referred to in the first part of this lecture. It calls for (1) Transformation of the whole of Tibet, including the eastern provinces of Kham and Amdo, into a Zone of *Ahimsa* (non-violence); (2) Abandonment of China's population transfer policy; (3) Respect for the Tibetan people's fundamental human rights and democratic freedoms; (4) Restoration and protection of Tibet's natural environment; and (5) Commencement of earnest negotiations on the future status of Tibet and of relations between the Tibetan and Chinese peoples. In the Strasbourg address I proposed that Tibet become a fully self-governing democratic political entity.

I would like to take this opportunity to explain the Zone of Ahimsa or peace sanctuary concept, which is the central element of the Five Point Peace Plan. I am convinced that it is of great importance not only for Tibet, but for peace and stability in Asia.

It is my dream that the entire Tibetan plateau should become a free refuge where humanity and nature can live in peace and in harmonious balance. It would be a place where people from all over the world could come to seek the true meaning of peace within themselves, away from the tensions and pressures of much of the rest of the world. Tibet could indeed become a creative center for the promotion and development of peace.

The following are key elements of the proposed Zone of Ahimsa:

—the entire Tibetan plateau would be demilitarized;

—the manufacture, testing, and stockpiling of nuclear weapons and other armaments on the Tibetan plateau would be prohibited;

—the Tibetan plateau would be transformed into the world's largest natural park or biosphere. Strict laws would be enforced to protect wildlife and plant life; the exploitation of natural resources would be carefully regulated so as not to damage relevant ecosystems; and a policy of sustainable development would be adopted in populated areas;

—the manufacture and use of nuclear power and other technologies which produce hazardous waste would be prohibited;

—national resources and policy would be directed towards the active promotion of peace and environmental protection. Organizations dedicated to the furtherance of peace and to the protection of all forms of life would find a hospitable home in Tibet;

—the establishment of international and regional organizations for the promotion and protection of human rights would be encouraged in Tibet.

Tibet's height and size (the size of the European Community), as well as its unique history and profound spiritual heritage make it ideally suited to fulfill the role of a sanctuary of peace in the strategic heart of Asia. It would also be in keeping with Tibet's historical role as a peaceful Buddhist nation and buffer region separating the Asian continent's great and often rival powers.

In order to reduce existing tensions in Asia, the President of the Soviet Union, Mr. [Mikhail] Gorbachev, proposed the demilitarization of Soviet-Chinese borders and their transformation into a "frontier of peace and good-neighborliness." The Nepal government had earlier proposed that the Himalayan country of Nepal, bordering on Tibet, should become a zone of peace, although that proposal did not include demilitarization of the country.

For the stability and peace of Asia, it is essential to create peace zones to separate the continent's biggest powers and potential adversaries. President Gorbachev's proposal, which also included a complete Soviet troop withdrawal from Mongolia, would help to reduce tension and the potential for confrontation between the Soviet Union and China. A true peace zone must, clearly, also be created to separate the world's two most populous states, China and India.

The establishment of the Zone of Ahimsa would require the withdrawal of troops and military installations from Tibet, which would enable India and Nepal also to withdraw troops and military installations from the Himalayan regions bordering Tibet. This would have to be achieved by international agreements. It would be in the best interest of all states in Asia, particularly China and India, as it would enhance their security, while reducing the economic burden of maintaining high troop concentrations in remote areas.

Tibet would not be the first strategic area to be demilitarized. Parts of the Sinai peninsula, the Egyptian territory separating Israel and Egypt, have been demilitarized for some time. Of course, Costa Rica is the best example of an entirely demilitarized country.

Tibet would also not be the first area to be turned into a natural preserve or biosphere. Many parks have been created throughout the world. Some very strategic areas have been turned into natural "peace parks." Two examples are the La Amistad park, on the Costa Rica–Panama border and the Si A Paz project on the Costa Rica–Nicaragua border.

When I visited Costa Rica earlier this year, I saw how a country can develop successfully without an army, to become a stable democracy committed to peace and the protection of the natural environment. This confirmed my belief that my vision of Tibet in the future is a realistic plan, not merely a dream.

Let me end with a personal note of thanks to all of you and our friends who are not here today. The concern and support which you have expressed for the plight of the Tibetans has touched us all greatly, and continues to give us courage to struggle for freedom and justice; not through the use of arms, but with the powerful weapons of truth and determination. I know that I speak on behalf of all the people of Tibet when I thank you and ask you not to forget Tibet at this critical time in our country's history. We too hope to contribute to the development of a more peaceful, more humane and more beautiful world. A future free Tibet will seek to help those in need throughout the world, to protect nature, and to promote peace. I believe that our Tibetan ability to combine spiritual qualities with a realistic and practical attitude enables us to make a special contribution in however modest a way. This is my hope and prayer.

In conclusion, let me share with you a short prayer which gives me great inspiration and determination:

For as long as space endures,
And for as long as living beings remain,
Until then may I, too, abide
To dispel the misery of the world.

Thank you.

"Free Speech Is Life Itself"

Salman Rushdie

Salman Rushdie, born in Bombay, India, in 1947, has
written a number of novels that have won critical ac-
claim. However, one novel, *The Satanic Verses*, published
in 1988, became the center of a continuing debate between defenders of freedom of speech versus the power
and influence of political and religious extremism. This
book, which explores questions of good and evil, religious faith and fanaticism, myth and reality, and the differences between Indian and British society, proved enormously controversial. Rushdie's portrayal of Islamic
history met with outrage by devout Muslims. Muslim religious and political leaders charged Rushdie with blasphemy for insulting both Mohammed, the prophet and
founder of Islam, and the Koran, the Muslim sacred text.
Riots broke out in India, Pakistan, and South Africa in
protest of the novel's publication. Iran's religious leader,
Ayatollah Ruhollah Khomeini, issued a *fatwa*, a special
decree that called for the execution of Rushdie and anyone associated with the publication. A dozen countries
banned its importation. A multimillion-dollar reward was
offered to anyone who assassinated Rushdie and his accomplices. The Iranian *fatwa* forced Rushdie into hiding.
During his confinement he moved from one safe house to
another. Guarded by British police, his public appearances were rare. Islamic terrorists bombed the British embassy in Pakistan as well as the stores that sold the book.
In the United States several stores were criticized when
they removed the book from their shelves. The novel's

From Salman Rushdie's speech delivered at the Columbia University School of
Journalism, December 11, 1991. Copyright © 1991 by Salman Rushdie. Reprinted
by permission of the author and his agents, the Wylie Agency.

Japanese translator was murdered, the Norwegian publisher shot, and the Italian translator stabbed.

Writers and leading intellectuals around the world came to Rushdie's defense. In December 1991, Columbia University's Graduate School of Journalism held a dinner in honor of both the two-hundredth anniversary of the First Amendment and one of its leading defenders in the twentieth century, retired Supreme Court justice William Brennan. The appearance and the following speech made by Rushdie surprised most of the audience in attendance.

In the following speech, Rushdie equates his situation with that of Western hostages that had recently been released from Lebanon. Rushdie strongly implies that because he is a novelist, society values him less than these hostages—otherwise, political leaders would do more to secure his safety from the Muslim extremists who have targeted him. In addition, Rushdie describes his attempts to make peace with the Muslims by explaining his concept of a more secular Muslim culture, only to find that such views are not tolerated under Islam in its current form. Rushdie concludes that he has no regrets about writing *The Satanic Verses* and insists that the book must be freely available in order to combat the forces of religious intolerance and defend the right of free speech.

In 1999, the Iran government assured the British government that the *fatwa* on Rushdie had been lifted. However, in 2001 an Iranian radical Islamic institution renewed the death sentence on Rushdie. The Islamic Propagation Organization stated, "The *fatwa* against the apostate Rushdie is irrevocable."

A hot-air balloon drifts slowly over a bottomless chasm, carrying several passengers. A leak develops; the balloon starts losing height. The pit, a dark yawn, comes closer. Good grief! The wounded balloon can bear just one passenger to safety; the many must be sacrificed to save the one! But who should live, who should die? And who could make such a choice?

In point of fact, debating societies everywhere regularly make such choices without qualms, for of course what I've described is the given situation of that evergreen favorite the balloon debate, in which, as the speakers argue over the relative merits and demerits of the well-known figures they have placed in disaster's mouth, the assembled company blithely accepts the faintly unpleasant idea that a human being's right to life is increased or diminished by his or her virtues or vices—that we may be born equal but thereafter our lives weigh differently in the scales.

It's only make-believe, after all. And while it may not be very nice, it does reflect how people actually think.

I have now spent over a thousand days in just such a balloon; but, alas, this isn't a game. For most of these thousand days, my fellow travelers included the Western hostages in the Lebanon and the British businessmen imprisoned in Iran and Iraq, Roger Cooper and Ian Richter. And I had to accept, and did accept, that for most of my countrymen and countrywomen, my plight counted for less than the others'. In any choice between us, I'd have been the first to be pitched out of the basket and into the abyss. "Our lives teach us who we are," I wrote at the end of my essay "In Good Faith." Some of the lessons have been harsh, and difficult to learn.

Trapped inside a metaphor, I've often felt the need to redescribe it, to change the terms. This isn't so much a balloon, I've wanted to say, as a bubble, within which I'm simultaneously exposed and sealed off. The bubble floats above and through the world, depriving me of reality, reducing me to an abstraction. For many people, I've ceased to be a human being. I've become an issue, a bother, an "affair." Bulletproof bubbles, like this one, are reality proof, too. Those who travel in them, like those who wear [British author J.R.R.] Tolkien's rings of invisibility, become wraith-like if they're not careful. They get lost. In this phantom space a man may become the bubble that encases him, and then one day— pop!—he's gone forever.

It's ridiculous—isn't it?—to have to say, "But I *am* a human being, unjustly accused, unjustly embubbled." Or is it I who am being ridiculous, as I call out from my bubble, "I'm still trapped in here, folks; somebody, please, get me out"?

Religious Persecution

Out there where you are, in the rich and powerful and lucky West, has it really been so long since religions persecuted people, burning them as heretics, drowning them as witches, that you can't recognize religious persecution when you see it? . . . The original metaphor has reasserted itself. I'm back in the balloon, asking for the right to live.

What is my single life worth? Despair whispers in my ear, "Not a lot." But I refuse to give in to despair.

I refuse to give in to despair, because I've been shown love as well as hatred. I know that many people do care, and are appalled by the crazy, upside-down logic of the post-*fatwa* world, in which a single novelist can be accused of having savaged or "mugged" a whole community, becoming its tormentor (instead of its tarred-and-feathered victim) and the scapegoat for all its discontents. Many people do ask, for example, "When a white pop star turned Islamic fanatic speaks approvingly about killing an Indian immigrant, how does the Indian immigrant end up being called the racist?"

Or, again, "What minority is smaller and weaker than a minority of one?"

I refuse to give in to despair even though, for a thousand days and more, I've been put through a degree course in worthlessness, my own personal and specific worthlessness. My first teachers were the mobs marching down distant boulevards, baying for my blood and finding, soon enough, their echoes on English streets. I could not understand the force that makes parents hang murderous slogans around their children's necks. I have learned to understand it. It burns books and effigies and thinks itself holy. But at first, as I watched the marchers, I felt them trampling on my heart.

Freedom of Thought Is Freedom from Religious Control

Once again, however, I have been saved by instances of fair-mindedness, of goodness. Every time I learn that a reader somewhere has been touched by *The Satanic Verses*, moved and entertained and stimulated by it, it arouses deep feelings in me. And there are more and more such readers nowadays, my postbag tells me, readers (including Muslims) who are willing to give my burned, spurned child a fair hearing at long last. Milan Kundera writes to say that he finds great tenderness towards Muslim culture in the book, and I'm stupidly grateful. A Muslim writes to say that in spite of the book's "shock tactics" its ideas about the birth of Islam are very positive; at once, I find myself wishing upon a star that her coreligionists may somehow, impossibly, come to agree with her.

Sometimes I think that, one day, Muslims will be ashamed of what Muslims did in these times, will find the "Rushdie affair" as improbable as the West now finds martyr burning. One day they may agree that—as the European Enlightenment demonstrated—freedom of thought is precisely freedom from religious control, freedom from accusations of blasphemy. Maybe they'll agree, too, that the row over *The Satanic Verses* was at bottom an argument about who should have power over the grand narrative, the story of Islam, and that that power must belong equally to everyone. That even if my novel were incompetent, its attempt to retell the story would still be important. That if I've failed, others must succeed, because those who do not have power over the story that dominates their lives, power to retell it, rethink it, deconstruct it, joke about it, and change it as times change, truly are powerless, because they cannot think new thoughts.

One day. Maybe. But not today.

Today, my education in worthlessness continues, and what Saul Bellow would call my "reality instructors" include the media pundit who suggests that a manly death would be better for me than hiding like a rat; the letter writer who points out that of course the trouble is that I *look* like the devil, and wonders if I have hairy shanks and cloven hooves; the "moderate" Muslim who writes to say that Muslims find it "revolting" when I speak about the Iranian death threats (it's not the *fatwa* that's revolting, you understand, but my mention of it); the rather more immoderate Muslim who tells me to "shut up," explaining that if a fly is caught in a spider's web, it should not attract the attention of the spider. I ask the reader to imagine how it might feel to be intellectually and emotionally bludgeoned, from a thousand different directions, every day for a thousand days and more.

What Is a Novelist Worth?

Back in the balloon, something longed-for and heartening has happened. On this occasion, mirabile dictu, the many have not been sacrificed but saved. That is to say, my companions, the Western hostages and the jailed businessmen, have by good fortune and the efforts of others managed to descend safely to earth and have been reunited with their families and friends, with their own, free lives. I rejoice for them and admire their courage, their resilience. And now I'm alone in the balloon.

Surely I'll be safe now? Surely now the balloon will drop safely towards some nearby haven, and I, too, will be reunited with my life? Surely it's my turn now?

But the balloon is over the chasm again; and it's still sinking. I realize that it's carrying a great deal of valuable freight. Trading relations, armaments deals, the balance of power in the Gulf—these and other matters of great moment are weighing down the balloon. I hear voices suggesting that if I stay aboard, this precious cargo will be endangered. The national interest is being redefined; am I being redefined out of it? Am I to be jettisoned, after all?

When Britain renewed relations with Iran at the United Nations in 1990, the senior British official in charge of the negotiations assured me in unambiguous language that something very substantial had been achieved on my behalf. The Iranians, laughing merrily, had secretly agreed to forget the *fatwa*. (The diplomat telling me the story put great stress on this cheery Iranian laughter.) They would "neither encourage nor allow" their citizens, surrogates, or proxies to act against me. Oh, how I wanted to believe that! But in the year and a bit that followed, we saw the *fatwa* restated in Iran, the bounty money doubled, the book's Italian translator severely wounded, its Japanese translator stabbed to death; there was news of an attempt to find and kill me by contract killers working directly for the Iranian government through its European embassies. Another such contract was successfully carried out in Paris, the victim being the harmless and aged ex-prime minister of Iran, Shapour Bakhtiar.

It seems reasonable to deduce that the secret deal made at the United Nations hasn't worked. Dismayingly, however, the talk as I write is all of improving relations with Iran still further, while the "Rushdie case" is described as a side issue.

Is this a balloon I'm in, or the dustbin of history?

Let me be clear: *there is nothing I can do to break this impasse.* The *fatwa* was politically motivated to begin with, it remains a breach of international law, and it can only be solved at the political level. To effect the release of the Western hostages in the Lebanon, great levers were moved; great forces were brought into play; for Mr. Richter, seventy million pounds in frozen Iraqi assets were "thawed." What, then, is a novelist under terrorist attack worth?

Despair murmurs, once again, "Not a plugged nickel."

But I refuse to give in to despair.

You may ask why I'm so sure there's nothing I can do to help myself out of this jam.

At the end of 1990, dispirited and demoralized, feeling abandoned, even then, in consequence of the British government's decision to patch things up with Iran, and with my marriage at an end, I faced my deepest grief, my unquenchable sorrow at having been torn away from, cast out of, the cultures and societies from which I'd always drawn my strength and inspiration—that is, the broad community of British Asians, and the broader community of Indian Muslims. I determined to make my peace with Islam, even at the cost of my pride. Those who were surprised and displeased by what I did perhaps failed to see that I was not some deracinated Uncle Tom Wog. To these people it was apparently incomprehensible that I should seek to make peace between the warring halves of the world, which were also the warring halves of my soul—and that I should seek to do so in a spirit of humility, instead of the arrogance so often attributed to me.

Conversations with Myself

In "In Good Faith" I wrote, "Perhaps a way forward might be found through the mutual recognition of [our] mutual

pain," but even moderate Muslims had trouble with this notion: what pain, they asked, could I possibly have suffered?
What was I talking about? As a result, the really important
conversations I had in this period were with myself.

I said, "Salman, you must send a message loud enough to
be heard all over the world. You must make ordinary Muslims see that you aren't their enemy, and make the West understand a little more of the complexity of Muslim culture."
It was my hope that Westerners might say, "Well, if he's the
one in danger, and yet he's willing to acknowledge the importance of his Muslim roots, then perhaps we ought to start
thinking a little less stereotypically ourselves." (No such
luck, though. The message you send isn't always the one
that's received.)

And I said to myself, "Admit it, Salman, the story of Islam has a deeper meaning for you than any of the other
grand narratives. Of course, you're no mystic, mister, and
when you wrote, 'I am not a Muslim,' that's what you meant.
No supernaturalism, no literalist orthodoxies, no formal
rules for you. But Islam doesn't have to mean blind faith. It
can mean what it always meant in your family, a culture, a
civilization, as open-minded as your grandfather was, as de-
lightedly disputatious as your father was, as intellectual and
philosophical as you like. Don't let the zealots make Muslim
a terrifying word," I urged myself; "remember when it meant
'family' and 'light.'"

I reminded myself that I had always argued that it was
necessary to develop the nascent concept of the secular Muslim, who, like the secular Jews, affirmed his membership of
the culture while being separate from the theology. I had recently read the contemporary Muslim philosopher Fouad
Zakariya's *Laïcité au Islamisme,* and been encouraged by
Zakariya's attempt to modernize Islamic thought. "But,
Salman," I told myself, "you can't argue from outside the debating chamber. You've got to cross the threshold, go inside
the room, and *then* fight for your humanized, historicized,
secularized way of being a Muslim." I recalled my near-
namesake, the twelfth-century philosopher ibn-Rushd (Aver-
roës), who argued that (to quote the great Arab historian Al-
bert Hourani), "not all the words of the Qu'ran should be

taken literally. When the literal meaning of Qu'ranic verses appeared to contradict the truths to which philosophers arrived by the exercise of reason, those verses needed to be interpreted metaphorically." But ibn-Rushd was a snob. Having propounded an idea far in advance of its time, he qualified it by saying that such sophistication was only suitable for the elite; literalism would do for the masses. "Salman," I asked myself, "is it time to pick up ibn-Rushd's banner and carry it forward—to say, nowadays such ideas are fit for everybody, for the beggar as well as the prince?"

It was with such things in mind—and with my thoughts in a state of some confusion and torment—that I spoke the Muslim creed before witnesses. But my fantasy of joining the fight for the modernization of Muslim thought, for freedom from the shackles of the Thought Police, was stillborn. It never really had a chance. Too many people had spent too long demonizing or totemizing me to listen seriously to what I had to say. In the West, some "friends" turned against me, calling me by yet another set of insulting names. Now I was spineless, pathetic, debased; I had betrayed myself, my cause; above all, I had betrayed *them*.

I also found myself up against the granite, heartless certainties of Actually Existing Islam, by which I mean the political and priestly power structure that presently dominates and stifles Muslim societies. Actually Existing Islam has failed to create a free society anywhere on earth, and it wasn't about to let me, of all people, argue in favor of one. Suddenly I was (metaphorically) among people whose social attitudes I'd fought all my life—for example, their attitudes about women (one Islamicist boasted to me that his wife would cut his toenails while he made telephone calls, and suggested I found such a spouse) or about gays (one of the imams I met in December 1990 was on TV soon afterwards, denouncing Muslim gays as sick creatures who brought shame on their families and who ought to seek medical and psychiatric help). Had I truly fallen in among such people? *That was not what I meant at all.*

Facing the utter intransigence, the philistine scorn of so much of Actually Existing Islam, I reluctantly concluded that there was no way for me to help bring into being the Muslim culture I'd dreamed of, the progressive, irreverent, skeptical, argumentative, playful, and *unafraid* culture which is what I've always understood as *freedom*. Not me, not in this lifetime, no chance. Actually Existing Islam, which has all but deified its Prophet, a man who always fought passionately against such deification, which has supplanted a priest-free religion by a priest-ridden one, which makes literalism a weapon and redescriptions a crime, will never let the likes of me in.

Ibn-Rushd's ideas were silenced in their time. And throughout the Muslim world today, progressive ideas are in retreat. Actually Existing Islam reigns supreme, and just as the recently destroyed "Actually Existing Socialism" of the Soviet terror state was horrifically unlike the utopia of peace and equality of which democratic socialists have dreamed, so also is Actually Existing Islam a force to which I have never given in, to which I cannot submit.

There is a point beyond which conciliation looks like capitulation. I do not believe I passed that point, but others have thought otherwise.

I have never disowned my book, nor regretted writing it. I said I was sorry to have offended people, because I had not set out to do so, and so I am. I explained that writers do not agree with every word spoken by every character they create—a truism in the world of books, but a continuing mystery to *The Satanic Verses's* opponents. I have always said that this novel has been traduced. Indeed, the chief benefit of my meeting with the six Islamic scholars on Christmas Eve, 1990, was that they agreed that the novel had no insulting motives. "In Islam, it is a man's intention that counts," I was told. "Now we will launch a worldwide campaign on your behalf to explain that there has been a great mistake." All this with much smiling and friendliness and handshaking. It was in this context that I agreed to suspend—not cancel—a paperback edition, to create what I called a space for reconciliation.

Free Speech Is the Whole Ball Game

Alas, I overestimated these men. Within days, all but one of them had broken their promises and recommenced to vilify me and my work as if we had not shaken hands. I felt (most probably I had been) a great fool. The suspension of the paperback began at once to look like a surrender. In the aftermath of the attacks on my translators, it looks even more craven. It has now been more than three years since *The Satanic Verses* was published; that's a long, long "space for reconciliation." Long enough. I accept that I was wrong to have given way on this point. *The Satanic Verses* must be freely available and easily affordable, if only because if it is not read and studied, then these years will have no meaning. Those who forget the past are condemned to repeat it.

"Our lives teach us who we are." I have learned the hard way that when you permit anyone else's description of reality to supplant your own—and such descriptions have been raining down on me, from security advisers, governments, journalists, archbishops, friends, enemies, mullahs—then you might as well be dead. Obviously, a rigid, blinkered, absolutist worldview is the easiest to keep hold of; whereas the fluid, uncertain, metamorphic picture I've always carried about is rather more vulnerable. Yet I must cling with all my might to that chameleon, that chimera, that shape-shifter, my own soul; must hold on to its mischievous, iconoclastic, out-of-step clown instincts, no matter how great the storm. And if that plunges me into contradiction and paradox, so be it; I've lived in that messy ocean all my life. I've fished in it for my art. This turbulent sea was the sea outside my bedroom window in Bombay. It is the sea by which I was born, and which I carry within me wherever I go.

"Free speech is a nonstarter," says one of my Islamic extremist opponents. No, sir, it is not. Free speech is the whole thing, the whole ball game. Free speech is life itself. That's the end of my speech from this ailing balloon. Now it's time to answer the question, What is my single life worth?

Is it worth more or less than the fat contracts and political treaties that are in here with me? Is it worth more or less than good relations with a country which, in April 1991, gave eight hundred women seventy-four lashes each for not wearing a veil; in which the eighty-year-old writer Mariam Firouz is still in jail, and has been tortured; and whose foreign minister says, in response to criticism of his country's lamentable human rights record, "International monitoring of the human rights situation in Iran should not continue indefinitely. . . . Iran could not tolerate such monitoring for long"?

You must decide what you think a friend is worth to his friends, what you think a son is worth to his mother, or a father to his son. You must decide what a man's conscience and heart and soul are worth. You must decide what you think a writer is worth, what value you place on a maker of stories, and an arguer with the world.

Ladies and gentlemen, the balloon is sinking into the abyss.

The State Must Allow Religious Freedom

John Paul II

As a young man, Pope John Paul II, born Karol Wojtyla
in Poland, witnessed the Nazi occupation of his country
and many of the horrors of that time. Since his election
as pope in 1978, he has attempted to repair the relationship between Catholics and Jews, greatly damaged as a
result of World War II. Although he is often criticized for
refusing to recognize and improve the status of women in
the Church and as laypeople, he has been a spokesperson
for prisoner's rights, social justice, and the freedom of
worship. He has worked more actively for those causes
on the international scene than any previous pope, particularly in countries of Latin America, Asia, and Africa.

The pope's visit to Cuba in 1998, when he gave the
following sermon, inspired people of all faiths in that
country which, like other communist countries, is
avowedly atheistic. In his sermon, the pope called on the
Cuban government to create an environment conducive
to the free worship of all faiths in both private and public
life. He states that while the state should not be founded
on religious ideology, government should not be completely devoid of spirituality.

The pope's visit contributed to a trend of loosening
restrictions on worship in Cuba. In 1990, Fidel Castro,
the president of Cuba, met with the evangelical Christians and lifted the prohibition on simultaneous membership in the Communist Party and a church. The govern-

---

From John Paul II's sermon at an open-air mass in Havana, Cuba, January 25,
1998.

ment also legalized meetings in private homes for religious worship and Bible study. In 1996, Castro made a historic visit to the Vatican. Following the pope's 1998 visit to Cuba, Christians were able to legally celebrate Christmas for the first time since communist rule began in 1959.

T he word of God calls us together to grow in faith and to celebrate the presence of the risen Lord in our midst, for "by one Spirit we were all baptized into one body" (1 Cor 12: 13), the Mystical Body of Christ which is the Church. Jesus Christ unites all the baptized. From him flows the fraternal love among Cuban Catholics and Catholics everywhere, since all are "the body of Christ and individually members of it" (1 Cor 12: 27). The Church in Cuba is not alone or isolated; rather, it is part of the Universal Church which extends throughout the whole world. . . .

The State Must Allow Freedom of Worship

"The Spirit of the Lord is upon me, because he has anointed me to preach good news to the poor" (Lk 4: 18). Every minister of God has to make his own these words spoken by Jesus in Nazareth. And so, as I come among you, I wish to bring you the Good News of hope in God. As a servant of the Gospel I bring you this message of love and solidarity which Jesus Christ, by his coming, offers to men and women in every age. In absolutely no way is this an ideology or a new economic or political system; rather, it is a *path of authentic peace, justice and freedom.*

The ideological and economic systems succeeding one another in the last two centuries have often encouraged conflict as a method, since their programmes contained the seeds of opposition and disunity. This fact profoundly affected their understanding of man and of his relations with others. Some of these systems also presumed to relegate religion to the merely private sphere, stripping it of any social influence or importance. In this regard, it is helpful to recall that *a modern State cannot make atheism or religion one of its political ordinances.* The State, while distancing itself from all extremes of fanaticism or secularism, should encourage a harmonious social climate and a suitable legislation which enables every person and every religious confession to live their faith freely, to express that faith in the context of public life and to count on adequate resources and opportunities to bring its spiritual, moral and civic benefits to bear on the life of the nation.

On the other hand, various places are witnessing the resurgence of a certain *capitalist neoliberalism* which subordinates the human person to *blind market forces* and conditions the development of peoples on those forces. From its centres of power, such neoliberalism often places unbearable burdens upon less favored countries. Hence, at times, *unsustainable economic programmes* are imposed on nations as a condition for further assistance. In the international community, we thus see *a small number of countries growing exceedingly rich at the cost of the increasing impoverishment of a great number of other countries;* as a result the wealthy grow ever wealthier, while the poor grow ever poorer.

In Seeking Justice We Cannot Hesitate

Dear brothers and sisters: *the Church is a teacher in humanity.* Faced with these systems, she presents *a culture of love and of life,* restoring hope to humanity, hope in the transforming power of love lived in the unity willed by Christ. For this to happen, it is necessary to follow *a path of reconciliation, dialogue and fraternal acceptance* of one's neighbour, of every human person. This can be called the social Gospel of the Church. The Church, in carrying out her mission, *sets before the world a new justice,* the justice of the kingdom of God (cf. Mt 6: 33). On various occasions I have spoken on social themes. It is necessary to keep speaking on these themes, as long as any injustice, however small, is present in the world; otherwise the Church would not be faithful to the mission entrusted to her by Christ. *At stake here is man,* the concrete human person. While times and situations may change, there are always people who need the voice of the Church so that their difficulties, their suffering and their distress may be known. Those who find themselves in these situations can be certain that they will not be betrayed, for the Church is with them and the Pope, in his heart and with his words of encouragement, embraces all who suffer injustice.

[A long burst of applause.]

I am not against applause because when you applaud the Pope can take a little rest!

On the threshold of the Year 2000, the teachings of Jesus maintain their full force. They are valid for all of you, dear brothers and sisters. In seeking the justice of the kingdom we cannot hesitate in the face of difficulties and misunderstandings. If the Master's call to justice, to service and to love is accepted as good news, then the heart is expanded, criteria are transformed and a culture of love and life is born. This is the great change which society needs and expects; and it can only come about if there is first a conversion of each individual heart, as a condition for the necessary changes in the structures of society.

"The Spirit of the Lord has sent me to proclaim release to the captives . . . to set at liberty those who are oppressed" (Lk 4: 18). The Good News of Jesus must be accompanied by a proclamation of freedom based on the solid foundation of truth: *"If you continue in my word, you are truly my disciples, and you will know the truth and the truth will make you free"* (Jn 8: 31-32). The truth of which Jesus speaks is not only the intellectual grasp of reality, but also *the truth about man* and his transcendent condition, *his rights and duties, his greatness and his limitations.* It is the same truth which Jesus proclaimed with his life, reaffirmed before Pilate and, by his silence, before Herod; it is the same truth that led him to his saving Cross and his glorious Resurrection.

A freedom which is not based on truth conditions man in such a way that he sometimes becomes the object and not the subject of his social, cultural, economic and political surroundings; this leaves him almost no initiative for his personal development. At other times that freedom takes on an individualistic cast and, with no regard for the freedom of others, imprisons man in his own egoism. *The attainment of freedom in responsibility is a duty which no one can shirk.* For Christians, *the freedom of the children of God* is not only a gift and a task, but its attainment also involves an invaluable witness and a genuine contribution to the journey towards the liberation of the whole human race. *This liberation cannot be reduced to its social and political aspects,* but rather reaches its fullness in the exercise of *freedom of conscience, the basis and foundation of all other human rights.*

To the crowds who were shouting: "The Pope is free and wants us all to be free", the Pope replied:

Yes, he lives with that freedom for which Christ has set you free.

For many of the political and economic systems operative today the greatest challenge is still that of *combining freedom and social justice, freedom and solidarity,* so that no one is relegated to a position of inferiority. *The Church's social doctrine* is meant to be a reflection and a contribution which can shed light on and reconcile the relationship between the inalienable rights of each individual and the needs of society, so that people can attain their profound aspirations and integral fulfilment in accordance with their condition as sons and daughters of God and citizens in society. Hence *the Catholic laity* should contribute to this fulfilment by the *application of the Church's social teachings in every sector* open to people of goodwill.

In the Gospel proclaimed today, justice is seen as intimately linked to truth. This is also evident in the *enlightened thinking of the Fathers of your country.* The Servant of God *Fr Félix Varela,* inspired by his Christian faith and his fidelity to the priestly ministry, sowed in the heart of the Cuban people the seeds of justice and freedom which he dreamed of seeing blossom in an independent Cuba.

Human Injustices Offend Virtue

The teaching of José Martí on love between all people had profoundly evangelical roots, and thus overcame the false conflict between faith in God and love and service to one's country. This great leader wrote: "Pure, selfless, persecuted, tormented, poetic and simple, the religion of the Nazarene enthralled all honourable men. . . . *Every people needs to be religious*. Not only as part of its essence, but for its own practical benefit it needs to be religious. . . . An irreligious people will die, because nothing in it encourages virtue. Human injustices offend virtue; it is necessary that heavenly justice guarantee it".

As everyone knows, *Cuba has a Christian soul* and this has brought her a *universal vocation*. Called to overcome isolation, she needs to open herself to the world and the world needs to draw close to Cuba, her people, her sons and daughters who are surely her greatest wealth. *This is the time to start out on the new paths* called for by the times of renewal which we are experiencing at the approach of the third millennium of the Christian era!

Dear brothers and sisters: *God has blessed this people with true educators of the national conscience*, clear and firm models of the Christian faith as the most effective support of virtue and love. Today the Bishops, with the priests, men and women religious and lay faithful, are striving to build bridges in order to bring minds and hearts closer together; they are fostering and strengthening peace, and *preparing the civilization of love and justice*. I am present among you *as a messenger of truth and hope*. For this reason I wish to repeat my appeal: *let Jesus Christ enlighten you; accept without reservation the splendour of his truth*, so that all can *set out on the path of unity through love and solidarity*, while avoiding exclusion, isolation and conflict, which are contrary to the will of God who is Love.

May the Holy Spirit enlighten by his gifts those who, in different ways, are responsible for the future of this people so close to my heart. And may Our Lady of Charity of El Cobre, Queen of Cuba, obtain for her children the gifts of peace, progress and happiness.

This wind today is very significant because wind symbolizes the Holy Spirit. "Spiritus spirat ubi vult; Spiritus vult spirare in Cuba". My last words are in Latin, because Cuba also has a Latin tradition: Latin America, Latin Cuba, Latin language! "Spiritus spirat ubi vult et vult Cubam"! Goodbye.

GREAT
SPEECHES
IN
HISTORY

Equal Rights: Emancipation for All

A Plea for Workers' Rights

Seth Luther

Seth Luther, born in Rhode Island in 1799, worked as a carpenter and as an advocate for labor reform. Primarily self-taught, in 1817 he traveled around the country visiting fourteen states. The class distinctions so present in his native New England seemed contradicted by the democratic frontier spirit that he observed in the West. Upon his return, he traveled throughout New England speaking up for workers' and children's rights. He wrote his first pamphlet "An Address to the Working-Men of New England," in 1832.

In the following speech, given in 1832 in several New England cities, Luther attacks the abuses of the factory system and the complicity of government leaders in failing to reform them. He decries the injustice of the working conditions in cotton mills, where women work "like slaves" for up to fourteen hours a day. Politicians have been deceived into thinking that working conditions are fair, he contends, by factory owners who clean up the factories prior to politicians' visits. In addition, he maintains, the press has supported the unjust system. Luther challenges the working class to claim their dignity and fight for their rights.

Our ears are constantly filled with the cry of national wealth, national American system, and American industry. . . .

From Seth Luther's speech advocating workers' rights delivered in several New England cities in 1832.

This cry is kept up by men who are endeavoring by all the means in their power to cut down the wages of our own people, and who send agents to Europe to induce foreigners to come here to underwork American citizens, to support American industry and the American system.

The whole concern (as now conducted) is as great a humbug as ever deceived any people. We see the system of manufacturing lauded to the skies; senators, representatives, owners, and agents of cotton mills using all means to keep out of sight the evils growing up under it. Cotton mills, where cruelties are practiced, excessive labor required, education neglected, and vice, as a matter of course, on the increase, are denominated 'the principalities of the destitute, the palaces of the poor.' . . . A member of the United States Senate seems to be extremely pleased with cotton mills; he says in the Senate, 'Who has not been delighted with the clockwork movements of a large cotton manufactory?' He had visited them often, and always with increased delight. He says the women work in large airy apartments well warmed; they are neatly dressed, with ruddy complexions and happy countenances, they mend the broken threads and replace the exhausted balls or broaches, and at stated periods they go to and return from their meals with a light and cheerful step. (While on a visit to that pink of perfection, Waltham, I remarked that the females moved with a very light step, and well they might, for the bell rung for them to return to the mill from their homes in nineteen minutes after it had rung for them to go to breakfast; some of these females boarded the largest part of half a mile from the mill.) And the grand climax is that at the end of the week, after working like slaves for thirteen or fourteen hours every day, 'they enter the temples of God on the Sabbath, and thank Him for all His benefits'—and the American system above all requires a peculiar outpouring of gratitude. We remark that whatever girls or others may do west of the Allegheny Mountains, we do not believe there can be a single person found east of those mountains who ever thanked God for permission to work in a cotton mill.

Without being obliged to attribute wrong or mercenary motives to the honorable senator (whose talents certainly must command respect from all, let their views in other respects be what they may), we remark that we think he was most grossly deceived by the circumstances of his visit. We will give our reasons in a few words spoken (in part) on a former occasion on this subject. It is well known to all that when honorables travel, timely notice is given of their arrival and departure in places of note. Here we have a case; the honorable senator from Kentucky is about to visit a cotton mill; due notice is given; the men, girls, and boys are ordered to array themselves in their best apparel. Flowers of every hue are brought to decorate the mill and enwreath the brows of the fair sex. If nature will not furnish the materials from the lap of summer, art supplies the deficiency. Evergreens mingle with the roses, the jasmine, and the hyacinth to honor the illustrious visitor, the champion, the very Goliath of the American system. He enters! Smiles are on every brow: No cowhide, or rod, or 'well-seasoned strap' is suffered to be seen by the honorable Senator or permitted to disturb the enviable happiness of the inmates of this almost celestial habitation. The honorable gentleman views with keen eye the 'clockwork'. He sees the rosy faces of the houris inhabiting this palace of beauty; he is in ecstasy—he is almost dumbfounded—he enjoys the enchanting scene with the most intense delight. For an hour or more (not fourteen hours) he seems to be in the regions described in Oriental song, his feelings are overpowered, and he retires, almost unconscious of the cheers which follow his steps; or if he hears the ringing shout, 'tis but to convince him that he is in a land of reality and not of fiction. His mind being filled with sensations, which, from their novelty, are without a name, he exclaims, 'tis a paradise; and we reply, if a cotton mill is a 'paradise', it is 'Paradise Lost' . . .

We Wish Nothing But Equal Rights

It has been said that the speaker is opposed to the American system. It turns upon one single point—if these abuses are the American system, he is opposed. But let him see *an* American system where education and intelligence are generally diffused, and the enjoyment of life and liberty secured to all; he then is ready to support such a system. But so long as our

government secures exclusive privileges to a very small part
of the community, and leaves the majority the 'lawful prey'
to avarice, so long does he contend against any 'system' so
exceedingly unjust and unequal in its operations. He knows
that we must have manufacturers. It is impossible to do without them; but he has yet to learn that it is necessary, or just,
that manufacturers must be sustained by injustice, cruelty, ignorance, vice, and misery; which is now the fact to a startling
degree. If what we have stated be true, and we challenge de-
nial, what must be done? Must we fold our arms and say, it
always was so and always will be? If we did so, would it not
almost rouse from their graves the heroes of our Revolution?
Would not the cold marble representing our beloved Washington start into life and reproach us for our cowardice? Let
the word be—onward! onward! We know the difficulties are
great, and the obstacles many; but, as yet, we 'know our
rights, and knowing, dare maintain'. We wish to injure no
man, and we are determined not to be injured as we have
been; we wish nothing but those equal rights which were designed for us all. And although wealth, and prejudice, and
slander, and abuse are all brought to bear on us, we have one
consolation—'We are the majority.'

One difficulty is a want of information among our own
class, and the higher orders reproach us for our ignorance;
but, thank God, we have enough of intelligence among us yet
to show the world that all is not lost.

Another difficulty among us is—the press has been almost
wholly, and is now in a great degree, closed upon us. We ven-
ture to assert that the press is bribed by gold in many instances; and we believe that if law had done what gold has accomplished, our country would, before this time, have been
deluged with blood. But workingmen's papers are multiply-
ing, and we shall soon, by the diffusion of intelligence, be enabled to form a front which will show all monopolists, and all
tyrants, that we are not only determined to have the name of
freemen, but that we will live freemen and die freemen.

Fellow citizens of New England, farmers, mechanics, and
laborers, we have borne these evils by far too long; we have
been deceived by all parties; we must take our business into
our own hands. Let us awake. Our cause is the cause of

truth—of justice and humanity. It must prevail. Let us be determined no longer to be deceived by the cry of those who produce nothing and who enjoy all, and who insultingly term us—the farmers, the mechanics, and laborers—the lower orders, and exultingly claim our homage for themselves, as the higher orders—while the Declaration of Independence asserts that 'All men are created equal.'

"Aren't I a Woman?"

Sojourner Truth

Due to the desire for greater freedom of people from all economic and cultural backgrounds in nineteenth century Europe and America, a groundswell of cultural and political change began to take place. The abolitionist and women's rights movements were instrumental in allowing people to gather and hear differing views on the status of women and African American people.

Among those indefatigable speakers for the rights of women and blacks was a preacher woman named Sojourner Truth. Originally born a slave named Isabella in upstate New York, she worked as a domestic slave after being sold, at the age of nine, and separated from her religiously devout parents. She was freed from slavery in 1828 as a result of the New York State Emancipation Act. She then supported herself and her children as a domestic in New York City. In 1843, she became a follower of a self-proclaimed messenger from God.

Upon her disillusionment with this preacher, she left New York City. During her travels she had a life-changing religious experience in which she began to hear heavenly voices. She decided then to take the name Sojourner Truth and devote her life to encouraging others to accept Jesus and to avoid sin. Her frequent opening line easily demanded people's attention: "Children, I talk to God and God talks to me!"

She drew large crowds wherever she preached, lecturing and performing songs throughout the Midwest and Northeast. She broadened her topics to include the abolition of slavery and prison reform, and she became an advocate for women's rights, a rare combination of efforts during that time. She attended both women's rights and

From Sojourner Truth's speech delivered to a women's rights convention in Akron, Ohio, May 29, 1851.

abolitionist conventions held in the northern states, even though white women often tried to prevent her from speaking, believing that she would hurt their cause.

In 1851 she addressed a women's rights convention in Akron, Ohio (it must be noted that recent scholarship has questioned whether this speech was ever actually given). Before she got up to the podium to speak, a white preacher had spoken to the crowd about why women were not equal to men. The renowned women's suffragist, Frances Gage, stood over the proceedings and recorded Truth's speech as well as the audience's reaction to her. She wrote: "Amid roars of applause, she returned to her corner, leaving more than one of us with streaming eyes, and hearts beating with gratitude. She had taken us up in her strong arms and carried us safely over the slough of difficulty turning the whole tide in our favor. I have never in my life seen anything like the magical influence that subdued the mobbish spirit of the day, and turned the sneers and jeers of an excited crowd into notes of respect and admiration. Hundreds rushed up to shake hands with her."

Despite continued abuse and arrest throughout her life, Sojourner Truth stood fast as a dynamic force to contend with on any subject related to fundamental human rights and dignity.

Well, children, where there is so much racket there must be something out o' kilter. I think that 'twixt the Negroes of the South and the women of the North all a-talking about rights, the white men will be in a fix pretty soon.

But what's all this here talking about? That man over there says that women need to be helped into carriages, and lifted over ditches, and to have the best place everywhere. Nobody ever helps me into carriages, or over mud puddles or gives me any best place, and aren't I a woman? Look at me! Look at my arm! I have plowed, and planted, and gathered into barns, and no man could head me—and aren't I a

woman? I could work as much and eat as much as a man
(when I could get it), and bear the lash as well—and aren't I
a woman? I have borne thirteen children and seen them almost all sold off into slavery, and when I cried out with a
mother's grief, none but Jesus heard—and aren't I a woman?

Then they talk about this thing in the head—what's this
they call it? That's it honey. What's that got to do with
woman's rights or Negroes' rights? If my cup won't hold but
a pint and yours holds a quart, wouldn't you be mean not to
let me have my little half-measure full?

Then that little man in black there, he says women can't
have as much rights as man, 'cause Christ wasn't a woman.
Where did your Christ come from? Where did your Christ
come from? From God and a woman. Man had nothing to
do with him.

If the first woman God ever made was strong enough to
turn the world upside down, all alone, these together ought
to be able to turn it back and get it right side up again; and
now they are asking to do it, the men better let them.

'Bliged to you for hearing on me, and now old Sojourner
hasn't got anything more to say.

"What, to the American Slave, Is Your Fourth of July?"

Frederick Douglass

Frederick Douglass was born Frederick Augustus Washington Bailey in 1818 in Maryland. He and his mother, Harriet Bailey, were slaves of Captain Aaron Anthony. In 1838, he fled slavery; disguised as a sailor, he boarded a train for Philadelphia. He eventually met up with Anna Murray, a free black woman whom he had courted in Baltimore. They moved to New Bedford, Massachusetts, where he worked as a common laborer.

In 1841, he attended a convention of the Massachusetts Anti-Slavery Society held by a Quaker on Nantucket Island. Abolitionist leaders William Lloyd Garrison, Lucretia Mott, and Wendell Phillips were in the audience. The society immediately engaged Douglass as a full-time speaker for the abolitionist movement. He quickly became one of the nation's most prominent antislavery figures. In 1845, he began a two-year lecture tour on the British Isles. Experiencing a new kind of social equality for the first time, Douglass bought his freedom from his owner, Thomas Auld, for fifty pounds.

Douglass returned to the United States as a freeman. He moved to Rochester, New York, one of the intellectual centers for the antislavery and women's suffrage movements, and began to publish a paper called the *North Star.* Devoted to the antislavery movement, it also

From Frederick Douglass's speech delivered July 5, 1852, in Rochester, New York.

advocated for the causes of black education, women's suffrage, and temperance.

On July 5, 1852, in Rochester, New York, Douglass gave a speech, excerpted here, that would have created a mob if heard in most towns. He focused on the issue of American slavery and the hypocrisy of a country that boasts of liberty for all while keeping a blind eye to so many who knew nothing of equality or freedom. His well-crafted use of rhetoric remains one of the most impressive of his day. He repeatedly states that he will not argue that a slave is a man because that is obvious. Of course, during the nineteenth century, to many this was not an obvious fact. Douglass knew this and used it to great effect in the development of this powerful speech.

Douglass insists that the celebration of the Fourth of July is a hollow mockery to slaves. As long as slavery exists, the nation's celebration of liberty is a meaningless sham. He strongly condemns slavery, stating, "There is not a nation on the earth guilty of practices more shocking and bloody than are the people of the United States at this very hour."

Fellow citizens, above your national, tumultuous joy, I hear the mournful wail of millions! whose chains, heavy and grievous yesterday, are, today, rendered more intolerable by the jubilee shouts that reach them. If I do forget, if I do not faithfully remember those bleeding children of sorrow this day, 'may my right hand forget her cunning, and may my tongue cleave to the roof of my mouth'! To forget them, to pass lightly over their wrongs, and to chime in with the popular theme would be treason most scandalous and shocking, and would make me a reproach before God and the world.

My subject, then, fellow citizens, is American slavery. I shall see this day and its popular characteristics from the slave's point of view. Standing there identified with the American bondman, making his wrongs mine. I do not hesitate to declare with all my soul that the character and conduct of this nation never looked blacker to me than on this Fourth of July! Whether we turn to the declarations of the past or to the professions of the present, the conduct of the nation seems equally hideous and revolting. America is false to the past, false to the present, and solemnly binds herself to be false to the future. Standing with God and the crushed and bleeding slave on this occasion, I will, in the name of humanity which is outraged, in the name of liberty which is fettered, in the name of the Constitution and the Bible which are disregarded and trampled upon, dare to call in question and to denounce, with all the emphasis I can command, everything that serves to perpetuate slavery—the great sin and shame of America! 'I will not equivocate; I will not excuse'; I will use the severest language I can command; and yet not one word shall escape me that any man, whose judgement is not blinded by prejudice, or who is not at heart a slaveholder, shall not confess to be right and just.

I Affirm the Equal Manhood of the Negro

But I fancy I hear someone of my audience say, 'It is just in this circumstance that you and your brother abolitionists fail to make a favorable impression on the public mind. Would you argue more and denounce less, would you persuade more and rebuke less, your cause would be much more likely to succeed.' But, I submit, where all is plain there is nothing to be argued. What point in the anti-slavery creed would you have me argue? On what branch of the subject do the people of this country need light? Must I undertake to prove that the slave is a man? That point is conceded already. Nobody doubts it. The slaveholders themselves acknowledge it in the enactment of laws for their government. They acknowledge it when they punish disobedience on the part of the slave. There are seventy-two crimes in the state of Virginia which, if committed by a black man (no matter how ignorant he be), subject him to the punishment of death; while only two of the same crimes will subject a white man to the like punishment. What is this but the acknowledgement that the slave is a moral, intellectual, and responsible being? The manhood of the slave is conceded. It is admitted in the fact that Southern statute books are covered with enactments forbidding, under severe fines and penalties, the teaching of the slave to read or to write. When you can point to any such laws in reference to the beasts of the field, then I may consent to argue the manhood of the slave. When the dogs in your streets, when the fowls of the air, when the cattle on your hills, when the fish of the sea and the reptiles that crawl shall be unable to distinguish the slave from a brute, then will I argue with you that the slave is a man!

For the present, it is enough to affirm the equal manhood of the Negro race. Is it not astonishing that, while we are plowing, planting, and reaping, using all kinds of mechanical tools, erecting houses, constructing bridges, building ships, working in metals of brass, iron, copper, silver, and gold; that, while we are reading, writing, and ciphering, acting as clerks, merchants, and secretaries, having among us lawyers, doctors, ministers, poets, authors, editors, orators, and teachers; that, while we are engaged in all manner of enterprises common to other men, digging gold in California, capturing the whale in the Pacific, feeding sheep and cattle on the hillside, living, moving, acting, thinking, planning, living in families as husbands, wives, and children, and, above all, confessing and worshiping the Christian's God, and looking hopefully for life and immortality beyond the grave, we are called upon to prove that we are men!

The Conscience of the Nation Must Be Roused

Would you have me argue that man is entitled to liberty? That he is the rightful owner of his own body? You have already declared it. Must I argue the wrongfulness of slavery? Is that a question for republicans? Is it to be settled by the rules of logic and argumentation, as a matter beset with great difficulty, involving a doubtful application of the principle of justice, hard to be understood? How should I look today, in the presence of Americans, dividing and subdividing a discourse, to show that men have a natural right to freedom? speaking of it relatively and positively, negatively and affirmatively? To do so would be to make myself ridiculous and to offer an insult to your understanding. There is not a man beneath the canopy of heaven that does not know that slavery is wrong for him.

What, am I to argue that it is wrong to make men brutes, to rob them of their liberty, to work them without wages, to keep them ignorant of their relations to their fellow men, to beat them with sticks, to flay their flesh with the lash, to load their limbs with irons, to hunt them with dogs, to sell them at auction, to sunder their families, to knock out their teeth, to burn their flesh, to starve them into obedience and submission to their masters? Must I argue that a system thus marked with blood, and stained with pollution, is wrong? No! I will not. I have better employment for my time and strength than such arguments would imply.

Frederick Douglass

What, then, remains to be argued? Is it that slavery is not divine; that God did not establish it; that our doctors of divinity are mistaken? There is blasphemy in the thought. That which is inhuman cannot be divine! Who can reason on such a proposition? They that can may; I cannot. The time for such argument is past.

At a time like this, scorching iron, not convincing argument, is needed. O! had I the ability, and could I reach the nation's ear, I would today pour out a fiery stream of biting ridicule, blasting reproach, withering sarcasm, and stern rebuke. For it is not light that is needed, but fire; it is not the gentle shower, but thunder. We need the storm, the whirlwind, and the earthquake. The feeling of the nation must be quickened; the conscience of the nation must be roused; the propriety of the nation must be startled; the hypocrisy of the nation must be exposed; and its crimes against God and man must be proclaimed and denounced.

What, to the American slave, is your Fourth of July? I answer: a day that reveals to him, more than all other days in the year, the gross injustice and cruelty to which he is the constant victim. To him, your celebration is a sham; your boasted liberty, an unholy license; your national greatness, swelling vanity; your sounds of rejoicing are empty and heartless; your denunciation of tyrants, brass-fronted impudence; your shouts of liberty and equality, hollow mockery; your prayers and hymns, your sermons and thanksgivings, with all your religious parade and solemnity, are, to him, mere bombast, fraud, deception, impiety, and hypocrisy—a thin veil to cover up crimes which would disgrace a nation of savages. There is not a nation of savages. There is not a nation on the earth guilty of practices more shocking and bloody than are the people of the United States at this very hour.

Go where you may, search where you will, roam through all the monarchies and despotisms of the Old World, travel through South America, search out every abuse, and when you have found the last, lay your facts by the side of the everyday practices of this nation, and you will say with me that, for revolting barbarity and shameless hypocrisy, America reigns without a rival.

The Emancipation of the Proletarian

Karl Marx

Born in Trier in the German Rhineland, Karl Marx studied law at Bonn and philosophy at the University of Berlin. In 1848, a year noted for revolution across continental Europe, he and Friedrich Engels (an English manufacturer) wrote and published *The Communist Manifesto*. While during his lifetime he was not well known, his writings have inspired many revolutions and political changes on behalf of the working class.

Marx lived in England from 1849 until his death, and during that time he spent most of his days writing in the British Museum library. His idealistic view that the revolt of the working class would abolish capitalism and improve the lives of people around the world has never been fully realized. However, his insights regarding the driving forces of economics in determining the well-being of the working class remains influential in political and humanitarian thought to this day, especially his theory of the negative impact of free trade upon the working classes.

The following speech was given on April 14, 1856, at the fourth anniversary celebration of the *People's Paper*, a Chartist movement paper that sympathized with the working class. Marx spoke of the inevitable success of the proletariat over the universal domination of "capital-rule and wages-slavery."

From Karl Marx's speech at the fourth anniversary celebration of the *People's Paper*, London, England, April 14, 1856.

The so-called revolutions of 1848 were but poor inci-
dents—small fractures and fissures in the dry crust of
European society. However, they denounced the abyss.
Beneath the apparently solid surface, they betrayed oceans of
liquid matter, only needing expansion to rend into fragments
continents of hard rock. Noisily and confusedly they proclaimed the emancipation of the Proletarian, i.e. the secret of
the 19th century, and of the revolution of that century.

That social revolution, it is true, was no novelty invented
in 1848. Steam, electricity, and the self-acting mule were rev-
olutionists of a rather more dangerous character than even
citizens Barbés, [Francois] Raspail and [Louis Auguste] Blan-
qui [all revolutionary figures; they led the first workers' revolt in France in 1848]. But, although the atmosphere in
which we live, weighs upon every one with a 20,000 lb.
force, do you feel it? No more than European society before
1848 felt the revolutionary atmosphere enveloping and
pressing it from all sides. There is one great fact, characteristic of this our 19th century, a fact which no party dares deny.

On the one hand, there have started into life industrial
and scientific forces, which no epoch of the former human
history had ever suspected. On the other hand, there exist
symptoms of decay, far surpassing the horrors recorded of
the latter times of the Roman Empire. In our days, everything
seems pregnant with its contrary: Machinery, gifted with the
wonderful power of shortening and fructifying human
labour, we behold starving and overworking it; The newfangled sources of wealth, by some strange weird spell, are
turned into sources of want; The victories of art seem bought
by the loss of character.

At the same pace that mankind masters nature, man
seems to become enslaved to other men or to his own infamy.
Even the pure light of science seems unable to shine but on the
dark background of ignorance. All our invention and progress
seem to result in endowing material forces with intellectual
life, and in stultifying human life into a material force.

This antagonism between modern industry and science
on the one hand, modern misery and dissolution on the other
hand; this antagonism between the productive powers and
the social relations of our epoch is a fact, palpable, over-

whelming, and not to be controverted. Some parties may wail over it; others may wish to get rid of modern arts, in order to get rid of modern conflicts. Or they may imagine that so signal a progress in industry wants to be completed by as signal a regress in politics. On our part, we do not mistake the shape of the shrewd spirit that continues to mark all these contradictions. We know that to work well the newfangled forces of society, they only want to be mastered by newfangled men—and such are the working men. They are as much the invention of modern time as machinery itself.

In the signs that bewilder the middle class, the aristocracy and the poor prophets of regression, we do recognise our brave friend, Robin Goodfellow [a character in William Shakespeare's *A Midsummer Night's Dream*], the old mole that can work in the earth so fast, that worthy pioneer—the Revolution. The English working men are the firstborn sons of modern industry. They will then, certainly, not be the last in aiding the social revolution produced by that industry, a revolution, which means the emancipation of their own class all over the world, which is as universal as capital-rule and wages-slavery. I know the heroic struggles the English working class have gone through since the middle of the last century—struggles less glorious, because they are shrouded in obscurity, and burked by the middleclass historian. To revenge the misdeeds of the ruling class, there existed in the middle ages, in Germany, a secret tribunal, called the "Vehmgericht." [Derived from the German words *vehme* (judgment, punishment) and *gericht* (count), Vehmgericht was a secret tribunal which exercised great power in Westphalia from the end of the twelfth to the middle of the sixteenth century.] If a red cross was seen marked on a house, people knew that its owner was doomed by the "Vehm." All the houses of Europe are now marked with the mysterious red cross.

History is the judge—its executioner, the proletarian.

"In Behalf of His Despised Poor"

John Brown

In 1849, John Brown, a white militant member of the American abolitionist movement, settled with his family in a black community founded in North Elba, New York. He later followed five of his sons to the Kansas Territory to assist antislavery forces struggling for control there. He began to believe that he had a divine mission to seek retribution on a mob of slavery sympathizers who in May 1856 sacked the town of Lawrence, Kansas.

In the spring of 1858, he gathered a group of blacks and whites in Chatham, Ontario, Canada, to announce his intent to create a refuge for escaped slaves in the Maryland and Virginia mountains. He gained the moral and financial support of several prominent abolitionists and in the summer of 1859 set up a headquarters in a Maryland farmhouse across the Potomac from Harper's Ferry, the site of a federal armory. On the night of October 16, he took the armory and rounded up sixty men of the area as hostages. Brown took this course of action in the hope that escaped slaves would join his rebellion and form an "army of emancipation" to liberate their fellow slaves. The following morning, although he held out against locals, he surrendered to a group of U.S. Marines who overpowered his hold. Brown was wounded and ten of his followers were killed. Although he was tried for murder, slave insurrection, and treason against the state and was convicted and hanged, he became a martyr for the cause. His actions are believed to have hastened the start of the Civil War.

From John Brown's speech to the court that condemned him, November 2, 1859.

Brown gave the following *ex tempore* speech after he was sentenced to hanging. He asserts that he was innocent of the act of treason and that he never intended to commit murder, destroy property, or incite rebellion. He states that he was guided by the "law of God" and by the Golden Rule. Brown also points out the irony of being condemned for his actions by those who seem to honor the Bible when he has been guided by its contents. He declares that if he had acted in the interests of the rich and powerful instead of the poor his actions would have been deemed "worthy of reward rather than punishment."

Brown continues to be cited as an example of someone willing to die for others in the cause of freedom. In 1906, nearly fifty years after his death, W.E.B. DuBois (a leading African American intellectual) gathered with other black leaders at Harper's Ferry to remember the events that took place there and the inspiration that Brown gave to the blacks then engaged in the fight for the right to vote. In his speech, considered one of the most significant in the history of the black struggle for equality, DuBois said: "We do not believe in violence, neither in the despised violence of the raid nor the lauded violence of the soldier. . . . But we do believe in John Brown, in that incarnate spirit of justice, that hatred of a lie, that willingness to sacrifice money, reputation, and life itself on the altar of right. And here on the scene of John Brown's martyrdom we reconsecrate ourselves, our honor, our property to the final emancipation of the race which John Brown died to make free."

I have, may it please the Court, a few words to say. In the first place, I deny everything but what I have all along admitted: of a design on my part to free slaves. I intended certainly to have made a clean thing of that matter, as I did last winter, when I went into Missouri and there took slaves without the snapping of a gun on either side, moving them through the country, and finally leaving them in Canada. I designed to have done the same thing again on a larger scale. That was all I intended. I never did intend murder, or treason, or the destruction of property, or to excite or incite slaves to rebellion, or to make insurrection.

I have another objection, and that is that it is unjust that I should suffer such a penalty. Had I interfered in the manner which I admit, and which I admit has been fairly proved—for I admire the truthfulness and candor of the greater portion of the witnesses who have testified in this case—had I so interfered in behalf of the rich, the powerful, the intelligent, the so-called great, or in behalf of any of their friends, either father, mother, brother, sister, wife or children, or any of that class, and suffered and sacrificed what I have in this interference, it would have been all right. Every man in this Court would have deemed it an act worthy of reward rather than punishment.

This Court acknowledges, too, as I suppose, the validity of the law of God. I see a book kissed, which I suppose to be the Bible, or at least the New Testament, which teaches me that all things whatsoever I would that men should do to me, I should do even so to them. It teaches me, further, to remember them that are in bonds as bound with them. I endeavored to act up to that instruction. I say I am yet too young to understand that God is any respecter of persons. I believe that to have interfered as I have done, as I have always freely admitted I have done, in behalf of His despised poor, I did no wrong, but right. Now, if it is deemed necessary that I should forfeit my life for the furtherance of the ends of justice, and mingle my blood further with the blood of my children and with the blood of millions in this slave country whose rights are disregarded by wicked, cruel, and unjust enactments, I say, let it be done.

I Feel No Guilt

Let me say one word further. I feel entirely satisfied with the treatment I have received on my trial. Considering all the circumstances, it has been more generous than I expected. But I feel no consciousness of guilt. I have stated from the first what was my intention, and what was not. I never had any design against the liberty of any person, nor any disposition to commit treason or incite slaves to rebel or make any general insurrection. I never encouraged any man to do so, but always discouraged any idea of that kind.

Let me say, also, in regard to the statements made by some of those who were connected with me, I hear it has been stated by some of them that I have induced them to join me. But the contrary is true. I do not say this to injure them, but as regretting their weakness. Not one but joined me of his own accord, and the greater part at their own expense. A number of them I never saw, and never had a word of conversation with, till the day they came to me, and that was for the purpose I have stated.

Now, I have done.

"Are Women Persons?"

Susan B. Anthony

Susan B. Anthony, born in Adams, Massachusetts, in 1820, grew up in an unusually freethinking household. Educated at home by her Quaker father and later at the Philadelphia Friends seminary, Anthony received more opportunities than most women of the early and mid-nineteenth century. In the early 1850s she devoted her energies to the temperance movement. In 1852 she was a delegate to a meeting held by the Sons of Temperance in Albany. She stood up to make a motion and was told "the sisters were not invited there to speak but to listen and learn." As a result of this event, and others like them, she began to see that only equal rights would allow women to really work for the social welfare of others. As she focused her energies on women's rights and the women's suffrage movement, Anthony became a leader in organizing women's rights conventions and lecture tours. After six years of campaigning in New York for married women's property rights, in 1860 the New York Legislature passed a law establishing the right of a married woman to own property separate from her husband. Her success in implementing political change fueled her efforts in the suffrage movement.

Anthony worked for the abolition of slavery as well as for women's rights. During the drafting of the Fourteenth Amendment, she tried to persuade those in power to include a provision to allow for the franchise of women as well as African Americans. She failed in this effort. In 1868, together with her lifelong friend Elizabeth Cady

From Susan B. Anthony's speech delivered in Rochester, New York, 1872.

Stanton (whom she had met in 1850) and Parker Pills-
bury, she founded a weekly women's suffrage paper, *The
Revolution*. The paper took a rather unorthodox stand in
that it opposed the Fourteenth and Fifteenth Amendments. Instead, it advocated for an amendment to the
Constitution that would declare "universal suffrage," regardless of sex or color. The journal also promoted equal
pay for the sexes and additional employment opportunities for women. These views created divisions which split
the suffrage movement into two organizations, the National Woman Suffrage Association (NWSA), the organization founded by Anthony and Stanton, and the American Woman Suffrage Association (AWSA), founded by
Lucy Stone and Julia Ward Howe. The AWSA favored a
state-by-state approach to gain voting rights. The movement remained split until 1890, when the National American Woman Suffrage Association formed to work toward
both state and national legislation.

In 1872, using a plan to test the legality of women's
suffrage under the Fifteenth Amendment in Rochester,
New York, Anthony registered to vote with fifteen other
women. Ratified in 1870, the Fifteenth Amendment
states: "The right of citizens of the United States to vote
shall not be denied or abridged by the United States or by
any State on account of race, color, or previous condition
of servitude." After registering, the women proceeded to
vote in the November presidential election. Two weeks
later Anthony was arrested for having violated the law.
Her trial was postponed and she took that opportunity to
vote again in elections held in March. Between November
and March she gave a number of speeches in an attempt
to educate people on women's right to vote. In the following speech she emphasizes that the Constitution does
not state, "We, the white male citizens; nor yet we, the
male citizens." Instead, it says, "We, the people of the
United States," which she believed included all the
people, not just some of the people.

Anthony devoted most of her life to trying to help
women achieve what we now assume to be a basic human right—the right to vote. In her lifetime she would

not see these efforts come to fruition in her country.
However, the year she died, a women's right to vote did
become legalized in Finland. The Nineteenth Amendment
to the U.S. Constitution, giving women the right to vote,
did not come into law until 1920, one hundred years after Anthony's birth.

Friends and fellow-citizens: I stand before you tonight
under indictment for the alleged crime of having voted
at the last presidential election, without having a lawful
right to vote. It shall be my work this evening to prove to you
that in thus voting, I not only committed no crime, but, instead, simply exercised my citizen's rights, guaranteed to me
and all United States citizens by the National Constitution,
beyond the power of any State to deny.

The preamble of the Federal Constitution says:

'We, the people of the United States, in order to form a
more perfect union, establish justice, insure domestic tran-
quillity, provide for the common defense, promote the general welfare, and secure the blessings of liberty to ourselves
and our posterity, do ordain and establish this Constitution
for the United States of America.'

It was we, the people; not we, the white male citizens; nor
yet we, the male citizens; but we, the whole people, who
formed the Union. And we formed it, not to give the blessings
of liberty, but to secure them; not to the half of ourselves and
the half of our posterity, but to the whole people—women as
well as men. And it is a downright mockery to talk to women
of their enjoyment of the blessings of liberty while they are denied the use of the only means of securing them provided by
this democratic-republican government—the ballot.

For any State to make sex a qualification that must ever result in the disfranchisement of one entire half of the people is
to pass a bill of attainder, or an *ex post facto* law, and is therefore a violation of the supreme law of the land. By it the blessings of liberty are forever withheld from women and their female posterity. To them this government has no just powers
derived from the consent of the governed. To them this gov-

ernment is not a democracy. It is not a republic. It is an odious aristocracy; a hateful oligarchy of sex; the most hateful aristocracy ever established on the face of the globe; an oligarchy of wealth, where the rich govern the poor. An oligarchy of learning, where the educated govern the ignorant, or even an oligarchy of race, where the Saxon rules the African, might be endured; but this oligarchy of sex, which makes father, brothers, husband, sons, the oligarchs over the mother and sisters, the wife and daughters of every household—which ordains all men sovereigns, all women subjects, carries dissension, discord and rebellion into every home of the nation.

Webster, Worcester and Bouvier all define a citizen to be a person in the United States, entitled to vote and hold office.

The only question left to be settled now is: Are women persons? And I hardly believe any of our opponents will have the hardihood to say they are not. Being persons, then, women are citizens; and no State has a right to make any law, or to enforce any old law, that shall abridge their privileges or immunities. Hence, every discrimination against women in the Constitutions and laws of the several states is today null and void, precisely as is every one against Negroes.

"I Have a Dream"

Martin Luther King Jr.

In 1954, when the U.S. Supreme Court determined that
segregation in public schools was illegal, racism was ram-
pant in the United States, especially in the South. Martin
Luther King Jr., a Baptist minister with a Ph.D., possessed
tremendous oratorical gifts and used them to lead the
way toward significant changes in the lives of African
Americans. He organized the Southern Christian Leadership Conference (SCLC), first in the South and later
throughout the country. Using the tactic of nonviolent resistance, he led many protests and marches during the
late 1950s and early 1960s. Despite their nonviolent nature, these demonstrations often provoked violent reac-
tions by police and bystanders, and protesters, including
King, were frequently arrested. On August 28, 1963,
King spearheaded the March on Washington, where he
gave his famous "I Have a Dream" speech to more than
two hundred thousand people.

King was awarded the Nobel Peace Prize in 1964. As
a result of his unrelenting efforts in mobilizing protests
and his ability to motivate people to speak out, many discriminatory laws were changed. Under the influence of
his leadership, the lives of African Americans and every
other minority were improved. Despite his assassination
on April 4, 1968, his words continue to inspire human
rights leaders around the world.

Five score years ago, a great American [Abraham Lin-
coln], in whose symbolic shadow we stand signed the
Emancipation Proclamation. This momentous decree

From Martin Luther King Jr., "I Have a Dream," speech delivered at the Lincoln
Memorial, Washington, DC, August 28, 1963. Copyright © Martin Luther King
1963; copyright renewed 1991 Coretta Scott King. Reprinted by arrangement with
the Estate of Martin Luther King Jr., c/o Writers House as agent for the proprietor.

came as a great beacon light of hope to millions of Negro slaves who had been seared in the flames of withering injustice. It came as a joyous daybreak to end the long night of captivity. But one hundred years later, we must face the tragic fact that the Negro is still not free.

One hundred years later, the life of the Negro is still sadly crippled by the manacles of segregation and the chains of discrimination. One hundred years later, the Negro lives on a lonely island of poverty in the midst of a vast ocean of material prosperity. One hundred years later, the Negro is still languishing in the corners of American society and finds himself an exile in his own land.

So we have come here today to dramatize an appalling condition. In a sense we have come to our nation's capital to cash a check. When the architects of our republic wrote the magnificent words of the Constitution and the Declaration of Independence, they were signing a promissory note to which every American was to fall heir.

This note was a promise that all men would be guaranteed the inalienable rights of life, liberty, and the pursuit of happiness. It is obvious today that America has defaulted on this promissory note insofar as her citizens of color are concerned. Instead of honoring this sacred obligation, America has given the Negro people a bad check which has come back marked "insufficient funds." But we refuse to believe that the bank of justice is bankrupt. We refuse to believe that there are insufficient funds in the great vaults of opportunity of this nation.

So we have come to cash this check—a check that will give us upon demand the riches of freedom and the security of justice. We have also come to this hallowed spot to remind America of the fierce urgency of now. This is no time to engage in the luxury of cooling off or to take the tranquilizing drug of gradualism. Now is the time to rise from the dark and desolate valley of segregation to the sunlit path of racial justice. Now is the time to open the doors of opportunity to all of God's children. Now is the time to lift our nation from the quicksands of racial injustice to the solid rock of brotherhood.

It would be fatal for the nation to overlook the urgency of the moment and to underestimate the determination of the

Negro. This sweltering summer of the Negro's legitimate discontent will not pass until there is an invigorating autumn of freedom and equality. Nineteen sixty-three is not an end, but a beginning. Those who hope that the Negro needed to blow off steam and will now be content will have a rude awakening if the nation returns to business as usual. There will be neither rest nor tranquility in America until the Negro is granted his citizenship rights.

The whirlwinds of revolt will continue to shake the foundations of our nation until the bright day of justice emerges. But there is something that I must say to my people who stand on the warm threshold which leads into the palace of justice. In the process of gaining our rightful place we must not be guilty of wrongful deeds. Let us not seek to satisfy our thirst for freedom by drinking from the cup of bitterness and hatred.

We must forever conduct our struggle on the high plane of dignity and discipline. We must not allow our creative protest to degenerate into physical violence. Again and again we must rise to the majestic heights of meeting physical force with soul force.

The marvelous new militancy which has engulfed the Negro community must not lead us to distrust of all white people, for many of our white brothers, as evidenced by their presence here today, have come to realize that their destiny is tied up with our destiny and their freedom is inextricably bound to our freedom.

We cannot walk alone. And as we walk, we must make the pledge that we shall march ahead. We cannot turn back. There are those who are asking the devotees of civil rights, "When will you be satisfied?" We can never be satisfied as long as our bodies, heavy with the fatigue of travel, cannot gain lodging in the motels of the highways and the hotels of the cities. We cannot be satisfied as long as the Negro's basic mobility is from a smaller ghetto to a larger one. We can never be satisfied as long as a Negro in Mississippi cannot vote and a Negro in New York believes he has nothing for which to vote. No, no, we are not satisfied, and we will not be satisfied until justice rolls down like waters and righteousness like a mighty stream.

I am not unmindful that some of you have come here out of great trials and tribulations. Some of you have come fresh from narrow cells. Some of you have come from areas where your quest for freedom left you battered by the storms of persecution and staggered by the winds of police brutality. You have been the veterans of creative suffering. Continue to work with the faith that unearned suffering is redemptive.

Let Freedom Ring

Go back to Mississippi, go back to Alabama, go back to Georgia, go back to Louisiana, go back to the slums and ghettos of our northern cities, knowing that somehow this situation can and will be changed. Let us not wallow in the valley of despair. I say to you today, my friends, that in spite of the difficulties and frustrations of the moment, I still have a dream. It is a dream deeply rooted in the American dream.

I have a dream that one day this nation will rise up and live out the true meaning of its creed: "We hold these truths to be self-evident: that all men are created equal." I have a dream that one day on the red hills of Georgia the sons of former slaves and the sons of former slaveowners will be able to sit down together at a table of brotherhood. I have a dream that one day even the state of Mississippi, a desert state, sweltering with the heat of injustice and oppression, will be transformed into an oasis of freedom and justice. I have a dream that my four children will one day live in a nation where they will not be judged by the color of their skin but by the content of their character. I have a dream today.

I have a dream that one day the state of Alabama, whose governor's lips are presently dripping with the words of interposition and nullification, will be transformed into a situation where little black boys and black girls will be able to join hands with little white boys and white girls and walk together as sisters and brothers. I have a dream today. I have a dream that one day every valley shall be exalted, every hill and mountain shall be made low, the rough places will be made plain, and the crooked places will be made straight, and the glory of the Lord shall be revealed, and all flesh shall see it together. This is our hope. This is the faith with which

I return to the South. With this faith we will be able to hew out of the mountain of despair a stone of hope. With this faith we will be able to transform the jangling discords of our nation into a beautiful symphony of brotherhood. With this faith we will be able to work together, to pray together, to struggle together, to go to jail together, to stand up for freedom together, knowing that we will be free one day.

This will be the day when all of God's children will be able to sing with a new meaning, "My country, 'tis of thee, sweet land of liberty, of thee I sing. Land where my fathers died, land of the pilgrim's pride, from every mountainside, let freedom ring." And if America is to be a great nation, this must become true. So let freedom ring from the prodigious hilltops of New Hampshire. Let freedom ring from the mighty mountains of New York. Let freedom ring from the heightening Alleghenies of Pennsylvania! Let freedom ring from the snowcapped Rockies of Colorado! Let freedom ring from the curvaceous peaks of California! But not only that; let freedom ring from Stone Mountain of Georgia! Let freedom ring from Lookout Mountain of Tennessee! Let freedom ring from every hill and every molehill of Mississippi. From every mountainside, let freedom ring.

When we let freedom ring, when we let it ring from every village and every hamlet, from every state and every city, we will be able to speed up that day when all of God's children, black men and white men, Jews and Gentiles, Protestants and Catholics, will be able to join hands and sing in the words of the old Negro spiritual, "Free at last! free at last! thank God Almighty, we are free at last!"

"We Want Equal Political Rights"

Nelson Mandela

Nelson Mandela was born in Umtata, a small town in the Transkei territory in South Africa. Renouncing his right to succeed his father as chief of the Tembu tribe in order to pursue a career in law, he studied at the University of the Witwatersrand in Johannesburg. In 1944, with Oliver Tambo and Walter F. Sisulu, he formed the Youth League of the African National Congress (ANC). In 1952, Mandela and Tambo opened the first South African law office owned by blacks.

Mandela led the armed struggle against the official South African policy of racial segregation, called *apartheid*. Apartheid was sanctioned by law in South Africa, and in 1948 legislation was passed to aggressively implement the policy. The government established residential and business areas for each of the three registered races: white, Bantu, and colored (mixed descent).

During the 1950s, Mandela was arrested several times but on each occasion he was acquitted or his sentence was suspended. However, in 1960, after the ANC was declared illegal, Mandela was indicted, and in 1962 he began to serve a five-year prison sentence for organizing illegal demonstrations. During his imprisonment, the ANC's headquarters were raided by police. Documents were found that described a guerilla campaign to overthrow the white-supremacist government. Mandela and seven others were sentenced to life in prison for acts of sabotage.

Protests by nonwhites, combined with international efforts, gradually moved the government toward modify-

From Nelson Mandela's speech at his trial in Rivonia, South Africa, 1964.

ing apartheid policies. The international efforts included
arms embargoes, trade sanctions, sports boycotts, withdrawal of overseas corporations, and political campaigns
in the United Nations. Beginning in 1985 the government
abolished many of the laws restricting nonwhites and offered to free Mandela if he agreed to renounce violence
upon his release. His principles remained firm; he refused
to leave prison (nor would the government be off the international political hook), until the government completely abolished apartheid and granted full political
rights to people of all colors.

The following are excerpts from a speech given by
Mandela at his trial in 1964, prior to being sentenced to
life imprisonment for conspiracy to overthrow the government. He states that the most important task at hand
is to end racial discrimination and the "attainment of
democratic rights." At that time, there were questions
about the relationship between the Communist Party and
the ANC. Mandela questions whether any role could be
played by communists given that they are opposed to a
parliamentary system. He states that as an African he
wants to be free "to borrow the best from the West and
from the East." Throughout the speech he focuses on a
number of human rights, including the need to end racial
discrimination, pointing out that black Africans have a
right to earn a living wage, to own land where they
work, and to have equal political rights.

While South Africa had been forced to withdraw
from the British Commonwealth in 1961 because of its
racial policies, it was not until the mid-1980s that economic sanctions were imposed. Human rights activists
began to campaign for Mandela's release. Worldwide
pressures prevailed upon South Africa, and in 1989 a
new government relaxed some of the apartheid laws. The
real symbol of change, however, was the legalization of
the ANC along with Mandela's release from prison, both
of which occurred in 1990. The ANC and the government entered into negotiations aimed at drafting a new
constitution that would grant political rights to blacks
and universal suffrage. Limited school integration began

in early 1991. By mid-1991 the last legal prop of apartheid, the 1950 act requiring the racial classification of all newborns, was repealed.

Also in 1991, negotiations began between Mandela and the president of South Africa, Frederik Willem de Klerk, to create a "new South Africa." The negotiations resulted in a provisional government formed between the National Party (NP) and the ANC. In May 1994 elections were held and monitored by over three thousand international observers. Mandela and de Klerk each ran for president. This was the first election in South Africa's history that allowed all races to vote and run for political office. The elections were considered chaotic, but essentially fair and reliable. The ANC and Mandela obtained 64.1 percent of the popular vote and 252 seats in the National Assembly. The NP and de Klerk, the former ruling party, won 20.5 percent of the popular vote and eighty-two seats. The Inkatha Freedom Party (IFP) and Mangosuthu Buthelezi, who at the last minute decided to participate in the elections, won 10.6 percent of the votes and forty-three seats. In four years, Mandela's status had changed from political prisoner to president of his country.

A t the outset, I want to say that the suggestion made by the state in its opening that the struggle in South Africa is under the influence of foreigners or Communists is wholly incorrect. I have done whatever I did, both as an individual and as a leader of my people, because of my experience in South Africa and my own proudly felt African background, and not because of what any outsider might have said.

In my youth in the Transkei I listened to the elders of my tribe telling stories of the old days. Amongst the tales they related to me were those of wars fought by our ancestors in defense of the fatherland. . . . I hoped then that life might offer me the opportunity to serve my people and make my own humble contribution to their freedom struggle. . . .

We felt that without violence there would be no way

open to the African people to succeed in their struggle against the principle of white supremacy. All lawful modes of expressing opposition to this principle had been closed by the legislation, and we were placed in a position in which we had to either accept a permanent state of inferiority or to defy the Government. . . . We first broke the law in a way which avoided any recourse to violence; when this form was legislated against, and when the Government resorted to a show of force to crush opposition to its policies, only then did we decide to answer violence with violence.

But the violence we chose to adopt was not terrorism. We who formed Umkonto were all members of the African National Congress, and had behind us the ANC tradition of nonviolence and negotiations as a means of solving political disputes. We believed that South Africa belonged to all the people who lived in it, and not to one group, be it black or white. We did not want an interracial war, and tried to avoid it to the last minute [Umkonto we Sizwe ("Spear of the Nation") was a guerrilla group founded by Mandela.]. . . .

This then was the plan: Umkonto was to perform sabotage, and strict instructions were given to its members, right from the start, that on no account were they to injure or kill people in planning or carrying out operations. . . .

I have denied that I am a Communist; and I think that in the circumstances I am obliged to state exactly what my political beliefs are. I have always regarded myself . . . as an African patriot. . . .

Today, I am attracted by the idea of a classless society, an attraction which springs in part from Marxist reading and in part from my admiration of the structure and organization of early African societies in this country. The land, then the main means of production, belonged to the tribe. There were no rich or poor and there was no exploitation.

I Have Been Influenced by the East and the West

It is true, as I have already stated, that I have been influenced by Marxist thought. But this is also true of many of the leaders of the new independent states. Such widely different persons as Gandhi, Nehru, Nkrumah and Nasser all acknowledge this. . . .

Indeed, for my own part, I believe that it is open to debate whether the Communist Party has any specific role to play at this particular stage of our political struggle. The basic task at the present moment is the removal of race discrimination and the attainment of democratic rights on the basis of the Freedom Charter. Insofar as that party furthers this task, I welcome its assistance. . . .

From my reading of Marxist literature and from conversations with Marxists, I have gained the impression that Communists regard the parliamentary system of the West as undemocratic and reactionary. But on the contrary, I am an admirer of such a system.

Magna Carta, the Petition of Rights and the Bill of Rights are documents held in veneration by democrats throughout the world.

I have great respect for British political institutions, and for the country's system of justice. I regard the British Parliament as the most democratic institution in the world, and the independence and impartiality of its judiciary never fail to arouse my admiration.

The American Congress, that country's doctrine of separation of powers, as well as the independence of its judiciary, arouse in me similar sentiments.

I have been influenced in my thinking by both West and East. All this has led me to feel that in my search for a political formula, I should be absolutely impartial and objective. I should tie myself to no particular system of society other than that of socialism. I must leave myself free to borrow the best from the West and from the East. . . .

The Government often answers its critics by saying that Africans in South Africa are economically better off than the inhabitants of the other countries in Africa. I do not know whether this statement is true and doubt whether any comparison can be made without having regard to the cost-of-living index in such countries.

But even if it is true, as far as the African people are concerned it is irrelevant. Our complaint is not that we are poor by comparison with people in other countries, but that we are poor by comparison with the white people in our own country, and that we are prevented by legislation from altering this imbalance.

To Be Treated with Dignity

The lack of human dignity experienced by Africans is the direct result of the policy of white supremacy. White supremacy implies black inferiority. Legislation designed to preserve white supremacy entrenches this notion.

Menial tasks in South Africa are invariably performed by Africans. When anything has to be carried or cleaned the white man will look around for an African to do it for him, whether the African is employed by him or not.

Because of this sort of attitude, whites tend to regard Africans as a separate breed. They do not look upon them as people with families of their own; they do not realize that they have emotions, that they fall in love like white people do, that they want to be with their wives and children like white people want to be with theirs, that they want to earn enough money to support their families properly, to feed and clothe them and send them to school. . . .

Africans want to be paid a living wage. Africans want to perform work they are capable of doing, and not work the Government declares them to be capable of. Africans want to be allowed to live where they obtain work, and not be endorsed out of an area because they were not born there.

Africans want to be allowed to own land in places where they work, and not be obliged to live in rented houses they can never call their own. Africans want to be part of the general population, and not confined to living in their own ghettos. . . .

Above all, we want equal political rights, because without them our disabilities will be permanent. I know this sounds revolutionary to the whites in this country, because the majority of voters will be Africans. This makes the white man fear democracy.

But this fear cannot be allowed to stand in the way of the only solution which will guarantee racial harmony and freedom for all. It is not true that the enfranchisement of all will result in racial domination. Political division, based on color, is entirely artificial, and when it disappears, so will the domination of one color group by another. The ANC has spent half a century fighting against racialism. When it triumphs it will not change that policy.

This then is what ANC is fighting. Their struggle is a truly national one. It is a struggle of the African people, inspired by their own suffering and their own experience. It is a struggle for the right to live.

During my lifetime I have dedicated myself to this struggle of the African people. I have fought against white domination, and I have fought against black domination. I have cherished the ideal of a democratic and free society in which all persons live together in harmony and with equal opportunities. It is an ideal I hope to live for and to achieve. But if needs be, it is an ideal for which I am prepared to die.

Chapter FOUR

GREAT
SPEECHES
IN
HISTORY

Human Rights: An International Responsibility

Adoption of the Declaration of Human Rights

Eleanor Roosevelt

Eleanor Roosevelt, born in 1884 as Anna Eleanor Roosevelt, was first known publicly as a politician's wife. However, she had been interested in and worked with the urban poor as a young woman prior to her marriage. Her husband, Franklin D. Roosevelt (also a distant cousin), served in many political positions, most notably as New York State governor and president of the United States. In 1921 he was stricken with polio and lost much of his mobility. As a result, Eleanor began to assist her physically disabled husband in political matters, serving as his "eyes and ears" by traveling throughout New York and the rest of the country to gauge the mood of the people. She also attended meetings and lectured on the governor's and, eventually, president's behalf. She initiated a number of bold and unprecedented steps: holding press conferences for women reporters only; making fact-finding trips; and promoting humanitarian efforts throughout the world. Through this work, she became widely respected as a person who both understood and felt the plight of common men and women.

As First Lady, Roosevelt was a keen civil rights activist during her husband's tenure as president and influenced much of his legislation in this and other areas. Perhaps one of her most enduring legacies was to serve as a U.S. delegate to the United Nations (UN) General Assembly from 1945 to 1951. In 1946, as elected chairman of

From Eleanor Roosevelt's speech delivered on the occasion of the adoption of the Universal Declaration of Human Rights in Paris, France, December 10, 1948.

the UN's Human Rights Commission (UNHRC), she
proved a formative influence on the early and final draft
of the UN's Universal Declaration of Human Rights
(UDHR). While many other members of the commission
were either scholars or experts on international law, after
years as a First Lady during and after World War II, she
contributed her well-honed diplomatic skills, determination, enthusiasm, and unflagging energy.

Envisioning a declaration with enduring principles
that would be perpetually recognized by all nations,
Eleanor Roosevelt was a strong advocate of true univer-
sality within the declaration. She was adamant that different conceptions of human rights be deliberated upon
during the composition of the UDHR. She later said, "We
wanted as many nations as possible to accept the fact
that men, for one reason or another, were born free and
equal in dignity and rights, that they were endowed with
reason and conscience, and should act toward one another in a spirit of brotherhood. The way to do that was
to find words that everyone would accept."

Roosevelt gave the following speech on December
10, 1948, in Paris, France, at the adoption ceremony of
the UDHR by the UN's General Assembly. It should be
noted that the historic "Four Freedoms" speech, given by
President Roosevelt at the beginning of the U.S. participation in World War II, informed and inspired much of the
thought and language in the final declaration. In her
speech, Mrs. Roosevelt clearly states the purpose and intent behind the declaration, which she hopes will become
"the international Magna Carta of all men everywhere."
She describes some of the processes involved in the drafting of the document as well as the vision behind it.
Above all, she clarifies that the declaration was meant to
inspire the future developments and goals of the United
Nations and to serve as a standard to strive toward
within the international community.

The UNHCR originally planned to draft an international human rights treaty. Instead, the commission decided to prepare a nonbinding declaration. The more
difficult task of drafting a binding treaty, called the In-

ternational Human Rights Covenants, was not com-
pleted until 1966. Today the UDHR together with the
Covenants are referred to as the International Bill of
Human Rights.

The long and meticulous study and debate of which this
Universal Declaration of Human Rights is the product
means that it reflects the composite views of the many
men and governments who have contributed to its formulation. Not every man nor every government can have what he
wants in a document of this kind. There are of course particular provisions in the declaration before us with which we
are not fully satisfied. I have no doubt this is true of other
delegations, but taken as a whole the Delegation of the
United States believes that this [is] a good document—even a
great document—and we propose to give it our full support.
The position of the United States on the various parts of the
declaration is a matter of record in the Third Committee.
[The Third (Social and Humanitarian) Committee of the
General Assembly of the UN met eighty-one times to discuss
the drafting of the declaration and proposed nearly seventy
amendments.] I shall not burden the Assembly, and particularly my colleagues of the Third Committee, with a restate-
ment of that position here.

Certain provisions of the declaration are stated in such
broad terms as to be acceptable only because of the limitations in article 29 providing for limitation on the exercise of
the rights for the purpose of meeting the requirements of
morality, public order, and the general welfare. An example
of this is the provision that everyone has the right of equal
access to the public service in his country. The basic principle
of equality and of nondiscrimination as to public employment is sound, but it cannot be accepted without limitations.
My government, for example, would consider that this is un-
questionably subject to limitation in the interest of public order and the general welfare. It would not consider that the
exclusion from public employment of persons holding sub-
versive political beliefs and not loyal to the basic principles

and practices of the constitution and laws of the country would in any way infringe upon this right.

Likewise, my Government has made it clear in the course of the development of the declaration that it does not consider that the economic and social and cultural rights stated in the declaration imply an obligation on governmental action. This was made quite clear in the Human Rights Commission text of article 23 which served as a so-called "umbrella" article to the articles on economic and social rights. We consider that the principle has not been affected by the fact that this article no longer contains a reference to the articles which follow it. This in no way affects our wholehearted support for the basic principles of economic, social, and cultural rights set forth in these articles.

An International Magna Carta

In giving our approval to the declaration today it is of primary importance that we keep clearly in mind the basic character of the document. It is not a treaty; it is not an international agreement. It is not and does not purport to be a statement of basic principles of law or legal obligation. It is a declaration of basic principles of human rights and freedoms, to be stamped with the approval of the General Assembly by formal vote of its members, and to serve as a common standard of achievement for all peoples of all nations.

We stand today at the threshold of a great event both in the life of the United Nations and in the life of mankind, that is the approval by the General Assembly of the Universal Declaration of Human Rights recommended by the Third Committee. This declaration may well become the international Magna Carta of all men everywhere. We hope its proclamation by the General Assembly will be an event comparable to the proclamation of the Declaration of the Rights of Man by the French people in 1789, the adoption of the Bill of Rights by the people of the United States, and the adoption of comparable declarations at different times in other countries.

At a time when there are so many issues on which we find it difficult to reach a common basis of agreement, it is a significant fact that 58 states [of the General Assembly] have found

While serving as a delegate to the United Nations, Eleanor Roosevelt was instrumental in drafting the Universal Declaration of Human Rights.

such a large measure of agreement in the complex field of human rights. This must be taken as testimony of our common aspiration first voiced in the Charter of the United Nations to lift men everywhere to a higher standard of life and to a greater enjoyment of freedom. Man's desire for peace lies behind this declaration. The realization that the flagrant violation of human rights by Nazi and Fascist countries sowed the seeds of the last world war has supplied the impetus for the work which brings us to the moment of achievement here today.

In a recent speech in Canada, Gladstone Murray said:

> The central fact is that man is fundamentally a moral being, that the light we have is imperfect does not matter so long as we are always trying to improve it . . . we are equal in sharing the moral freedom that distinguishes us as men. Man's status makes each individual an end in himself. No man is by nature simply the servant of the state or of another man . . . the ideal and fact of freedom—and not technology—are the true distinguishing marks of our civilization.

This declaration is based upon the spiritual fact that man must have freedom in which to develop his full stature and through common effort to raise the level of human dignity. We have much to do to fully achieve and to assure the rights set forth in this declaration. But having them put before us with the moral backing of 58 nations will be a great step forward.

As we here bring to fruition our labors on this Declaration of Human Rights, we must at the same time rededicate ourselves to the unfinished task which lies before us. We can now move on with new courage and inspiration to the completion of an international covenant on human rights and of measures for the implementation of human rights.

In conclusion I feel that I cannot do better than to repeat the call to action by Secretary [of State George C.] Marshall in his opening statement to this Assembly:

"Let this third regular session of the General Assembly approve by an overwhelming majority the Declaration of Human Rights as a statement of conduct for all; and let us, as Members of the United Nations, conscious of our own short-comings and imperfections, join our effort in all faith to live up to this high standard."

"Peace, Progress, Human Rights"

Andrei Sakharov

Andrei Sakharov, born in Moscow in 1921, gained early
recognition as one of the Soviet Union's most brilliant
physicists. Sakharov, with other prominent physicists,
helped to develop advances in nuclear weaponry. In
1949, he worked on the research team that succeeded in
testing an atomic bomb. Next, the team created a hydrogen bomb. Thus, Sakharov was often called "the father
of the hydrogen bomb." As a result of these achievements, in 1953, at the age of thirty-two, Sakharov
became the youngest scientist elected to the prestigious
Soviet Academy of Sciences.

In the 1950s, Sakharov continued to work as a research scientist but became increasingly concerned about
the negative effects of nuclear weapons upon the environment. Between 1958 and 1962, he repeatedly wrote private letters to President Nikita Khrushchev objecting to
the Soviet atomic testing. After privately criticizing Soviet
policies during Khrushchev's years, he began to speak out
publicly when Leonid Brezhnev and Alexei Kosygin were
in power.

Sakharov's political involvement came to a turning
point in 1968, when Soviet troops invaded Czechoslova-
kia. During this crisis, he wrote an essay, entitled
"Progress, Coexistence, and Intellectual Freedom,"
which asked for freedom of thought and discussion. The
essay, which was smuggled out of the country and published by the *New York Times*, ended Sakharov's distin-
guished scientific career.

From Andrei Sakharov's speech on acceptance, in absentia, of the Nobel Prize in
Physics in Oslo, Norway, 1975. Reprinted by permission of the Nobel Foundation.

In 1970, Sakharov organized and led a human rights
movement to help educate Soviet citizens about their
rights provided within the Soviet Constitution. His reputation as a peace activist and dissident grew during the
1970s, and in 1975 he received the Nobel Prize. However, the government denied him permission to leave the
country to accept it. The following speech, given by his
wife, Yelena, outlines his many concerns about the global
environment, poverty, overpopulation, the politicization
of the United Nations, and numerous human rights
abuses within the Soviet Union. He speaks about the responsibility of all nations to allow free discussion across
borders between scientists and other intellectuals. In addition, he strongly advocates the liberation of political prisoners in all countries and addresses the dangers of an increasingly polarized world. Peaceful coexistence and
human progress are not possible, he insists, unless citizens of all nations are afforded basic human rights such
as a free press and the right to travel and live where one
chooses—rights that were often denied in the Soviet
Union at that time.

Peace, progress, human rights—these three goals are in-
dissolubly linked: it is impossible to achieve one of
them if the others are ignored. This idea provides the
main theme of my lecture.

I am deeply grateful that this great and significant award,
the Nobel Peace Prize, has been given to me, and that I have
the opportunity of addressing you here today. I was particularly gratified at the Committee's citation, which stresses the
defense of human rights as the only sure basis for genuine
and lasting international cooperation. This idea is very important to me; I am convinced that international trust, mutual understanding, disarmament, and international security
are inconceivable without an open society with freedom of
information, freedom of conscience, the right to publish, and
the right to travel and choose the country in which one
wishes to live. I am also convinced that freedom of con-

science, together with other civic rights, provides both the basis for scientific progress and a guarantee against its misuse to harm mankind, as well as the basis for economic and social progress, which in turn is a political guarantee making the effective defense of social rights possible. At the same time I should like to defend the thesis of the original and decisive significance of civic and political rights in shaping the destiny of mankind. This view differs essentially from the usual Marxist theory, as well as from technocratic opinions, according to which only material factors and social and economic conditions are of decisive importance. (But in saying this, of course, I have no intention of denying the importance of people's material welfare.). . .

There is a great deal to suggest that mankind, at the threshold of the second half of the twentieth century, entered a particularly decisive and critical historical era.

Nuclear missiles exist capable in principle of annihilating the whole of mankind; this is the greatest danger threatening our age. Thanks to economic, industrial, and scientific advances, so-called "conventional" arms have likewise grown incomparably more dangerous, not to mention chemical and bacteriological instruments of war.

Progress and the Polarization of Mankind

There is no doubt that industrial and technological progress is the most important factor in overcoming poverty, famine, and disease. But this progress leads at the same tine to ominous changes in the environment in which we live and to the exhaustion of our natural resources. Thus, mankind faces grave ecological dangers.

Rapid changes in traditional forms of life have resulted in an unchecked demographic explosion which is particularly noticeable in the developing countries of the Third World. The growth in population has already created exceptionally complicated economic, social, and psychological problems and will in the future inevitably pose still more serious problems. In many countries, particularly in Asia, Africa, and Latin America, the lack of food will be an overriding factor in the lives of many hundreds of millions of people, who from the moment of birth are condemned to a wretched existence on the starvation level. Moreover, future prospects are menacing, and in the opinion of many specialists, tragic, despite the undoubted success of the "green revolution."

But even in the developed countries, people face serious problems. These include the pressure resulting from excessive urbanization, all the changes that disrupt the community's social and psychological stability, the incessant pursuit of fashion and trends, overproduction, the frantic, furious tempo of life, the increase in nervous and mental disorders, the growing number of people deprived of contact with nature and of normal human lives, the dissolution of the family and the loss of simple human pleasures, the decay of the community's moral and ethical principles, and the loss of faith in the purpose of life. Against this background there is a whole host of ugly phenomena: an increase in crime, in alcoholism, in drug addiction, in terrorism, and so forth. The imminent exhaustion of the world's resources, the threat of overpopulation, the constant and deep-rooted international, political, and social problems are making a more and more forceful impact on the developed countries too, and will deprive—or at any rate threaten to deprive—a great many people who are accustomed to abundance, affluence, and creature comforts.

However, in the pattern of problems facing the world today a more decisive and important role is played by the global political polarization of mankind, which is divided into the so-called First World (conventionally called the Western world), the Second (socialist), and the Third (the developing countries). Two powerful socialist states, in fact, have become mutually hostile totalitarian empires, in which a single party and the state exercise immoderate power in all spheres of life. They possess an enormous potential for expansion, striving to increase their influence to cover large areas of the globe. One of these states—the Chinese People's Republic—has reached only a relatively modest stage of economic development, whereas the other—the Soviet Union—by exploiting its unique natural resources, and by taxing to the utmost the powers of its inhabitants and their ability to suffer continued privation, has built up a tremendous war potential and a relatively high—though one-sided—economic development. But in the Soviet Union, too, the people's standard of living is low, and civic rights are more restricted than in less socialist countries. Highly complicated global problems also affect the Third World, where relative economic stagnation goes hand in hand with growing international political activity.

Moreover, this polarization further reinforces the serious dangers of nuclear annihilation, famine, pollution of the environment, exhaustion of resources, overpopulation, and dehumanization.

Progress Is Indispensable

If we consider this complex of urgent problems and contradictions, the first point that must be made is that any attempt to reduce the tempo of scientific and technological progress, to reverse the process of urbanization, to call for isolationism, patriarchal ways of life, and a renaissance based on ancient national traditions, would be unrealistic. Progress is indispensable, and to halt it would lead to the decline and fall of our civilization.

Not long ago we were unfamiliar with artificial fertilizers, mechanized farming, chemical pesticides, and intensive agricultural methods. There are voices calling for a return to more traditional and possibly less dangerous forms of agriculture. But can this be accomplished in a world in which hundreds of millions of people are suffering from hunger? On the contrary, there is no doubt that we need increasingly intensive methods of farming, and we must spread modern methods all over the world, including the developing countries.

We cannot reject the idea of a spreading use of the results of medical research or the extension of research in all its branches, including bacteriology and virology, neurophysiology, human genetics, and gene surgery, no matter what potential dangers lurk in their abuse and the undesirable social consequences of this research. This also applies to research in the creation of artificial intelligence systems, research involving behavior, and the establishment of a unified system of global communication, systems for selecting and storing information, and so forth. It is quite clear that in the hands of irresponsible bureaucratic authorities operating secretly, all this research may prove exceptionally dangerous, but at the same time it may prove extremely important and necessary to mankind, if it is carried out under public supervision and discussion and socio-scientific analysis. We cannot reject wider application of artificial materials, synthetic food, or the modernization of every aspect of life; we cannot obstruct growing automation and industrial expansion, irrespective of the social problems these may involve.

We cannot condemn the construction of bigger nuclear power stations or research into nuclear physics, since energetics is one of the bases of our civilization. . . .

We cannot cease interplanetary and intergalactic space research, including the attempts to intercept signals from civilizations outside our own earth. The chance that such experiments will prove successful is probably small, but precisely for this reason the results may well be tremendous.

I have mentioned only a few examples. In actual fact all important aspects of progress are closely interwoven; none of them can be discarded without the risk of destroying the entire structure of our civilization. Progress is indivisible. But intellectual factors play a special role in the mechanism of progress. Underestimating these factors is particularly widespread in the socialist countries, probably due to the populist-ideological dogmas of official philosophy, and may well result in distortion of the path of progress or even its cessation and stagnation.

Intellectual Freedom and Trust Between Nations

Progress is possible and innocuous only when it is subject to the control of reason. The important problems involving environmental protection exemplify the role of public opinion, the open society, and freedom of conscience. The partial liberalization in our country after the death of Stalin made it possible to engage in public debate on this problem during the early 1960s. But an effective solution demands increased tightening of social and international control. The military application of scientific results and controlled disarmament are an equally critical area, in which international confidence depends on public opinion and an open society. The example I gave involving the manipulation of mass psychology is already highly topical, even though it may appear farfetched.

Freedom of conscience, the existence of an informed public opinion, a pluralistic system of education, freedom of the press, and access to other sources of information—all these are in very short supply in the socialist countries. This situation is a result of the economic, political, and ideological monism which is characteristic of these nations. At the same time these conditions are a vital necessity, not only to avoid all witting or unwitting abuse of progress, but also to strengthen it.

An effective system of education and a creative sense of heredity from one generation to another are possible only in an atmosphere of intellectual freedom. Conversely, intellectual bondage, the power and conformism of a pitiful bureaucracy, acts from the very start as a blight on humanistic fields of knowledge, literature, and art and results eventually in a general intellectual decline, the bureaucratization and formalization of the entire system of education, the decline of scientific research, the thwarting of all incentive to creative work, stagnation, and dissolution.

In the polarized world the totalitarian states, thanks to détente, today may indulge in a special form of intellectual parasitism. And it seems that if the inner changes that we all consider necessary do not take place, those nations will soon be forced to adopt an approach of this kind. If this happens, the danger of an explosion in the world situation will merely increase. Cooperation between the Western states, the socialist nations, and the developing countries is a vital necessity for peace, and it involves exchanges of scientific achievements, technology, trade, and mutual economic aid, particularly where food is concerned. But this cooperation must be based on mutual trust between open societies, or—to put it another way—with an open mind, on the basis of genuine equality and not on the basis of the democratic countries' fear of their totalitarian neighbors. If that were the case, cooperation would merely involve an attempt at ingratiating oneself with a formidable neighbor. But such a policy would merely postpone the evil day, soon to arrive anyway and, then, ten times worse. . . . Détente can only be assured if from the very outset it goes hand in hand with continuous openness on the part of all countries, an aroused sense of public opinion, free exchange of information, and absolute respect in all countries for civic and political rights. In short: in addition to détente in the material sphere, with disarmament and trade, détente should take place in the intellectual and ideological sphere. . . .

I should also emphasize that I consider it particularly important for United Nations armed forces to be used more generally for the purpose of restricting armed conflicts between states and ethnic groups. I have a high regard for the United Nations role, and I consider the institution to be one of mankind's most important hopes for a better future. Recent years have proved difficult and critical for this organization. I have written on this subject in *My Country and the World,* but after it was published, a deplorable event took place: the General Assembly adopted—without any real debate—a resolution declaring Zionism a form of racism and racial discrimination. Zionism is the ideology of a national rebirth of the Jewish people after two thousand years of diaspora, and it is not directed against any other people. The adoption of a resolution of this kind has damaged the prestige of the United Nations. But despite such motions, which are frequently the result of an insufficient sense of responsibility among leaders of some of the UN's younger members, I believe nevertheless that the organization may sooner or later be in a position to play a worthy role in the life of mankind, in accordance with its Charter's aims.

Let me now address one of the central questions of the present age, the problem of disarmament. . . . It is imperative to promote confidence between nations, and carry out measures of control with the aid of international inspection groups. This is only possible if détente is extended to the ideological sphere, and it presupposes greater openness in public life. I have stressed the need for international agreements to limit arms supplies to other states, special agreements to halt production of new weapons systems, treaties banning secret rearmament, the elimination of strategically unbalancing factors, and in particular a ban on multi-warhead nuclear missiles. . . .

Soviet Human Rights Abuses: No Improvement

Regarding the problem of human rights, I should like to speak mainly of my own country. During the months since the Helsinki Conference there has been no real improvement in this direction. In fact there have been attempts on the part of hard-liners to "give the screw another turn," in international exchange of information, the freedom to choose the country in which one wishes to live, travel abroad for studies, work, or health reasons, as well as ordinary tourist travel. To illustrate my assertion, I should like to give you a few examples—chosen at random and without any attempt to provide a complete picture.

You all know, even better than I do, that children from Denmark can get on their bicycles and cycle off to the Adriatic. No one would ever suggest that they were "teenage spies." But Soviet children are not allowed to do this! I am sure you are familiar with analogous examples.

The UN General Assembly, influenced by the socialist states, has imposed restrictions on the use of satellites for international TV transmissions. Now that the Helsinki Conference has taken place, there is every reason to deal afresh with this problem. For millions of Soviet citizens this is an important and interesting matter.

In the Soviet Union there is a severe shortage of artificial limbs and similar aids for invalids. But no Soviet invalid, even though he may have received a formal invitation from a foreign organization, is allowed to travel abroad in response to such an invitation.

Soviet newsstands rarely offer non-Communist newspapers, and it is not possible to buy every issue of Communist periodicals. Even informative magazines like *Amerika* are in very short supply. They are on sale only at a small number of newsstands; and are immediately snapped up by eager buyers.

Any person wishing to emigrate from the Soviet Union

must have a formal invitation from a close relative. For many this is an insoluble problem—for 300,000 Germans, for example, who wish to go to West Germany. (The emigration quota for Germans is 5,000 a year, which means that one might be forced to wait for sixty years!) The situation for those who wish to be reunited with relatives in Socialist countries is particularly tragic. There is no one to plead their case, and in such circumstances the arbitrary behavior of the authorities knows no bounds.

The freedom to travel and the freedom to choose where one wishes to work and live are still violated in the case of millions of collective farm workers, and in the situation of hundreds of thousands of Crimean Tatars, who thirty years ago were cruelly and brutally deported from the Crimea and who to this day have been denied the right to return to their homeland.

The Helsinki Accord confirms the principle of freedom of conscience. However, a relentless struggle will have to be carried on if the provisions of this agreement are to be realized in practice. In the Soviet Union today many thousands of people are both judicially and extra-judicially persecuted for their convictions: for their religious faith and their desire to bring up their children in a religious spirit, or for reading and disseminating—often only to a few acquaintances—literature of which the state disapproves, but which from the standpoint of ordinary democratic practice is absolutely legitimate. On the moral plane, there is particular gravity in the persecution of persons who have defended other victims of unjust treatment, who have worked to publish and, in particular, to distribute information regarding both the persecution and trials of persons with deviant opinions and the conditions in places of imprisonment.

It is unbearable to consider that at the very moment we are gathered together in this hall on this festive occasion hundreds and thousands of prisoners of conscience are suffering from undernourishment, as the result of year-long hunger, of an almost total lack of proteins and vitamins in their diet, of a shortage of medicines (there is a ban on the sending of vitamins and medicines to inmates), and of overexertion. They shiver from cold, damp, and exhaustion in ill-lit dungeons, where they are forced to wage a ceaseless struggle for their human dignity and to maintain their convictions against the "indoctrination machine," in fact against the destruction of their souls. The special nature of the concentration-camp system is carefully concealed. The sufferings a handful have undergone, because they exposed the terrible conditions, provide the best proof of the truth of their allegations and accusations. Our concept of human dignity demands an immediate change in this system for all imprisoned persons, no matter how guilty they may be. But what about the sufferings of the innocent? Worst of all is the hell that exists in the special psychiatric clinics in Dnepropetrovsk, Sytchevka, Blagoveshchensk, Kazan, Chernyakhovsk, Orel, Leningrad, Tashkent. . . .

A final solution to persecutions can be based on international agreement—amnesty for political prisoners, for prisoners of conscience in prisons, internment camps, and psychiatric clinics as set forth in a UN General Assembly resolution. This proposal involves no intervention in the internal affairs of any country. It would apply to every state on the same basis—to the Soviet Union, to Indonesia, to Chile, to the Republic of South Africa, to Spain, to Brazil, and to every other country. Since the protection of human rights has been proclaimed in the United Nations Declaration of Human Rights, there can be no reason to call this issue a matter of purely internal or domestic concern. In order to achieve this goal, no efforts can be too great, however long the road may seem. And that the road is long was clearly shown during the recent session of the United Nations, in the course of which the United States moved a proposal for political amnesty, only to withdraw it after attempts had been made by a number of countries to expand the scope of the amnesty. I much regret what took place. A problem cannot be removed from circulation. I am profoundly convinced that it would be better to liberate a certain number of people—even though they might be guilty of some offense or other—than to keep thousands of innocent people locked up and exposed to torture.

Without losing sight of an overall solution of this kind, we must fight against injustice and the violation of human rights for every individual person separately. Much of our future depends on this.

We Need Reform, Not Revolution

In struggling to defend human rights we ought, I am convinced, first and foremost to protect the innocent victims of regimes installed in various countries, without demanding the destruction or total condemnation of these regimes. We need reform, not revolution. We need a flexible, pluralist, tolerant society, which selectively and experimentally can foster a free, undogmatic use of the experiences of all kinds of social systems. What is détente? What is rapprochement? We are concerned not with words, but with a willingness to create a better and more decent society, a better world order.

Thousands of years ago human tribes suffered great privations in the struggle to survive. It was then important not only to be able to handle a club, but also to possess the ability to think intelligently, to take care of the knowledge and experience garnered by the tribe, and to develop the links that would provide cooperation with other tribes. Today the human race is faced with a similar test. In infinite space many civilizations are bound to exist, among them societies that may be wiser and more "successful" than ours. I support the cosmological hypothesis which states that the development of the universe is repeated in its basic characteristics an infinite number of times. Further, other civilizations, including more "successful" ones, should exist an infinite number of times on the "preceding" and the "following" pages of the Book of the Universe. Yet we should not minimize our sacred endeavors in this world, where, like faint glimmers in the dark, we have emerged for a moment from the nothingness of dark unconsciousness into material existence. We must make good the demands of reason and create a life worthy of ourselves and of the goals we only dimly perceive.

Neutrality Is a Sin

Elie Wiesel

Elie Wiesel survived the Holocaust and came to the
United States from his native Romania in 1956. He proceeded to dedicate his life in bearing witness to Nazi
genocide through his novels, nonfiction writings, and
speeches given around the world. In the process, he has
become an outspoken advocate for human rights.

After World War II, a number of countries began to
see the importance of international responsibility for and
responses to the acts of individual countries. Through an
extensive international effort, Nazi criminals who orches-
trated crimes against the Jews and others were captured
and put on trial in Nuremberg, Germany. During the
same period of time, motivated to avoid the possibility of
another world war, the international community gathered
to create the United Nations Charter and, soon thereafter,
the Universal Declaration of Human Rights (an addition
to the Charter).

In 1985, President Ronald Reagan planned a visit to
West Germany to acknowledge the importance of that
country's membership in the alliance of free nations. As
part of the ceremonies, a visit to a cemetery in Bitburg,
Germany, was planned. It was discovered that several
members of Hitler's Waffen SS, notorious for their anti-
Semitism, were buried there. The president of West Germany, Helmut Kohl, made it known that he and his
country would be highly offended if the president can-
celled his trip to this cemetery. President Reagan went
ahead with the visit, but turned his back on the Nazi
graves. Just prior to his trip to Germany, he awarded Elie

From Elie Wiesel's speech on acceptance of the Congressional Gold Medal of
Achievement at the White House, April 19, 1985, as reprinted in *From the King-
dom of Memory*, by Elie Wiesel. Copyright © 1990 by Elirion Associates, Inc.
Reprinted by permission of Georges Borchardt, Inc.

Wiesel a national medal of achievement in recognition of his activities as then chairman of the U.S. Holocaust Memorial Council. This provided Wiesel an opportunity to publicly object to the visit on a very significant date, April 19, the same day in 1943 when the Warsaw Ghetto rose up against the Nazis without any international support. Wiesel states that it is a sin for nations to remain neutral when other nations are committing atrocities such as those committed during the Holocaust.

M r. President, . . . I am grateful to you for the medal. But this medal is not mine alone. It belongs to all those who remember what SS killers have done to their victims.

It was given to me by the American people for my writings, teaching and for my testimony. When I write, I feel my invisible teachers standing over my shoulders, reading my words and judging their veracity. And while I feel responsible for the living, I feel equally responsible to the dead. Their memory dwells in my memory.

Forty years ago, a young man awoke, and he found himself an orphan in an orphaned world. What have I learned in the last forty years? Small things. I learned the perils of language and those of silence. I learned that in extreme situations when human lives and dignity are at stake, neutrality is a sin. It helps the killers, not the victims. I learned the meaning of solitude, Mr. President. We were alone, desperately alone.

Today is April 19, and April 19, 1943, the Warsaw Ghetto rose in arms against the onslaught of the Nazis. They were so few and so young and so helpless. And nobody came to their help. And they had to fight what was then the mightiest legion in Europe. Every underground received help except the Jewish underground. And yet they managed to fight and resist and push back those Nazis and their accomplices for six weeks. And yet the leaders of the free world, Mr. President, knew everything and did so little, or nothing, or at least nothing specifically to save Jewish children from death. You spoke of Jewish children, Mr. President. One million

Jewish children perished. If I spent my entire life reciting their names, I would die before finishing the task.

Mr. President, I have seen children, I have seen them being thrown in the flames alive. Words, they die on my lips. So I have learned, I have learned, I have learned the fragility of the human condition.

And I am reminded of a great moral essayist. The gentle and forceful Abe Rosenthal, having visited Auschwitz, once wrote an extraordinary reportage about the persecution of Jews, and he called it "Forgive them not, Father, for they knew what they did."

I have learned that the Holocaust was a unique and uniquely Jewish event, albeit with universal implications. Not all victims were Jews. But all Jews were victims. I have learned the danger of indifference, the crime of indifference. For the opposite of love, I have learned, is not hate, but indifference. Jews were killed by the enemy but betrayed by their so-called allies, who found political reasons to justify their indifference or passivity.

But I have also learned that suffering confers no privileges. It all depends what one does with it. And this is why survivors, of whom you spoke, Mr. President, have tried to teach their contemporaries how to build on ruins, how to invent hope in a world that offers none, how to proclaim faith to a generation that has seen it shamed and mutilated. And I believe, we believe, that memory is the answer, perhaps the only answer.

A few days ago, on the anniversary of the liberation of Buchenwald, all of us, Americans, watched with dismay and anger as the Soviet Union and East Germany distorted both past and present history.

I Belong to a Traumatized Generation

Mr. President, I was there. I was there when American liberators arrived. And they gave us back our lives. And what I felt for them then nourishes me to the end of my days and will do so. If you only knew what we tried to do with them then. We who were so weak that we couldn't carry our own lives, we tried to carry them in triumph.

Mr. President, we are grateful to the American army for liberating us. We are grateful to this country, the greatest democracy in the world, the freest nation in the world, the moral nation, the authority in the world. And we are grateful, especially, to this country for having offered us haven and refuge, and grateful to its leadership for being so friendly to Israel.

And, Mr. President, do you know that the ambassador of Israel, who sits next to you, who is my friend, and has been for so many years, is himself a survivor? And if you knew all the causes we fought together for the last thirty years, you should be prouder of him. And we are proud of him.

And we are grateful, of course, to Israel. We are eternally grateful to Israel for existing. We needed Israel in 1948 as we need it now. And we are grateful to Congress for its continuous philosophy of humanism and compassion for the underprivileged.

And as for yourself, Mr. President, we are so grateful to you for being a friend of the Jewish people, for trying to help the oppressed Jews in the Soviet Union. And to do whatever we can to save [Anatoly] Shcharansky and Abe Stolar and Iosif Begun and [Andrey] Sakharov and all the dissidents who need freedom. And of course, we thank you for your support of the Jewish state of Israel.

But, Mr. President, I wouldn't be the person I am, and you wouldn't respect me for what I am, if I were not to tell you also of the sadness that is in my heart for what happened during the last week. And I am sure that you, too, are sad for the same reasons.

What can I do? I belong to a traumatized generation. And to us, as to you, symbols are important. And furthermore, following our ancient tradition, and we are speaking about Jewish heritage, our tradition commands us "to speak truth to power."

So may I speak to you, Mr. President, with respect and admiration, of the events that happened?

That Place Is Not Your Place

We have met four or five times. And each time I came away enriched, for I know of your commitment to humanity.

And therefore I am convinced, as you have told us earlier when we spoke, that you were not aware of the presence of SS graves in the Bitburg cemetery. Of course you didn't know. But now we all are aware.

May I, Mr. President, if it's possible at all, implore you to do something else, to find a way, to find another way, another site? That place, Mr. President, is not your place. Your place is with the victims of the SS.

Oh, we know there are political and strategic reasons, but this issue, as all issues related to that awesome event, transcends politics and diplomacy.

The issue here is not politics, but good and evil. And we must never confuse them.

For I have seen the SS at work. And I have seen their victims. They were my friends. They were my parents.

Mr. President, there was a degree of suffering and loneliness in the concentration camps that defies imagination. Cut off from the world with no refuge anywhere, sons watched helplessly their fathers being beaten to death. Mothers watched their children die of hunger. And then there was Mengele and his selections. Terror, fear, isolation, torture, gas chambers, flames, flames rising to the heavens.

But, Mr. President, I know and I understand, we all do, that you seek reconciliation. And so do I, so do we. And I too wish to attain true reconciliation with the German people. I do not believe in collective guilt, nor in collective responsibility. Only the killers were guilty. Their sons and daughters are not.

And I believe, Mr. President, that we can and we must work together with them and with all people. And we must work to bring peace and understanding to a tormented world that, as you know, is still awaiting redemption.

I thank you, Mr. President.

The Rights of Indigenous People

Rigoberta Menchú Tum

Born in 1959 to an Indian peasant family and raised in the Quiche branch of the Mayan culture in Guatemala, Rigoberta Menchú Tum became involved in social reform activities through the Catholic Church. As a teenager, she gained prominence in the women's rights movement. Tum grew up during a time of civil war in Guatemala, which lasted from 1960 until 1996. Her father, Vicente, was imprisoned and tortured for allegedly having participated in the execution of a local plantation owner. After being released, he became politically active and joined the Committee of the Peasant Union (CUC). In 1979, Tum also joined the CUC. Within two years her father, brother, and mother were tortured and murdered by opposition leaders. In 1981 Tum fled to exile in Mexico, which marked the beginning of a new phase in her life. She became an exiled resistance organizer, fighting against the oppression in Guatemala and supporting the struggle for Indian peasant peoples' rights.

The civil war took a heavy toll on Guatemala's indigenous people. In 1999, the Guatemalan Historical Clarification Commission, an independent body authorized by the peace accords that ended the war, concluded that more than 90 percent of the atrocities committed during the war were the work of the army and its paramilitary creations, the Patrullas de Autodefensa Civil, commonly known as PACs. The commission termed these atrocities "acts of genocide" against the Mayan population. Seventy percent of the population of Guatemala is

From Rigoberta Menchú Tum's Nobel Peace Prize acceptance speech delivered December 10, 1992, in Oslo, Norway. Reprinted by permission of the Nobel Foundation.

Mayan. More than two hundred thousand were killed before the war's end. A million more became refugees, chiefly in southern Mexico, and two hundred thousand more were internally displaced. On the government side, a million Guatemalans were engaged in the conflict, most of them in local PACs. In a population of eleven million, then, nearly two and a half million were directly affected by the war. By an official estimate, the war also created some forty thousand orphans.

Over the years, Rigoberta Menchú Tum has become widely known as a leading advocate of Indian rights in Guatemala and around the world. In 1992, she was awarded the Nobel Peace Prize for her efforts, and the United Nations subsequently declared 1993 *The Year of Indigenous Peoples*. The following speech was given by Tum in 1992 upon her acceptance of the Nobel Peace Prize. The speech was delivered in English, despite the fact that Tum is a non-native speaker of English. When Tum gave this speech, the Guatemalan war continued. Tum laments the five hundred years of oppression that she believes indigenous people have suffered in the Americas and calls for increased Indian participation in society and government. In addition, she deplores the state of human rights in Guatemala and calls for an end to forced military conscription, forced exodus, and restrictions on free movement.

I feel a deep emotion and pride for the honour of having been awarded the Nobel Peace Prize for 1992. A deep personal feeling and pride for my country and its very ancient culture. For the values of the community and the people to which I belong, for the love of my country, of Mother Nature. Whoever understands this respects life and encourages the struggle that aims at such objectives.

I consider this Prize not as an award to me personally, but rather as one of the greatest conquests in the struggle for peace, for the Human Rights and for the rights of the indigenous people who, along all these 500 years, have been split, fragmented, as well as the victims of genocides, repression and discrimination. . . .

It is also a tribute to the Centro-American people who still search for their stability, for the structuring of their future, and the path for their development and integration, based on civil democracy and mutual respect.

The importance of this Nobel Prize has been demonstrated by all the congratulations received from everywhere, from Heads of Government—practically all the American Presidents—to the organizations of the indigenous people and of Human Rights, from all over the world. In fact, what they see in this Nobel Prize is not only a reward and a recognition to a single person, but a starting point for hard struggle towards the achievement of those vindications that remain to be complied with.

As a contrast, and paradoxically, it was actually in my own country where I met, on the part of some people, the strongest objections, reserve and indifference, for the award of the Nobel Prize to this Quiche Indian. Perhaps because in Latin America, it is precisely in Guatemala where the discrimination towards natives, towards women, and the repression of the longing for justice and peace, are more deeply rooted in certain social and political sectors.

Under the present circumstances, in this convulsed and complex world, the decision of the Norwegian Nobel Peace Prize Committee to award this honourable distinction to me, reflects the awareness of the fact that, in this way, courage and strength is given to the struggle for peace, reconciliation and justice; to the struggle against racism, cultural discrimination, hence contributing to the achievement of harmonious coexistence between our people.

With deep pain, on one side, but with satisfaction on the other, I have to inform you that the Nobel Peace Prize 1992 will have to remain temporarily in Mexico City, in a kind of wake-waiting for peace in Guatemala. Because there are no political conditions in my country that would indicate or make me foresee a prompt and just solution. The satisfaction and gratitude are due to the fact that Mexico, our wonderful neighbour country, that has been so dedicated and interested, that has made such great efforts in respect of the negotiations that are being conducted to achieve peace, that has received and admitted so many refugees and exiled Guatemalans, has given us a place in the Museo del Templo Mayor (the cradle of the ancient Aztecas) so that the Nobel Prize may remain there, until peaceful and safe conditions are established in Guatemala to place it there, the land of the Quetzal.

When evaluating the overall significance of the award of the Peace Prize, I would like to say some words on behalf of all those whose voice cannot be heard or who have been repressed for having spoken in the manner of an opinion, of all those who have been marginalized, who have been discriminated, who live in poverty, in need, of all those who are the victims of repression and violation of human rights. Those who, nevertheless, have endured through centuries, who have not lost their conscience, the quality of determination and hope.

The Civilization of the Mayas

Please allow me, ladies and gentlemen, to say some words about my country and the Civilization of the Mayas. The Maya people developed and spread geographically through some 300,000 square km; they occupied parts of the South of Mexico, Belize, Guatemala, as well as Honduras and El Salvador; they developed a very rich civilization in the area of political organization, as well as in social and economic fields; they were great scientists in the fields of mathematics, astronomy, agriculture, architecture and engineering; they were great artists in the fields of sculpture, painting, weaving and carving.

The Mayas discovered the mathematic zero value, at about the same time that it was discovered in India and later passed on to the Arabs. Their astronomic forecasts based on mathematic calculations and scientific observations were amazing, and still are. They prepared a calendar more accurate than the Gregorian, and in the field of medicine they performed intra-cranial surgical operations.

One of the Maya books, saved from destruction by the conquerors, known as *Códice de Dresden*, contains the results of an investigation on eclipses as well a table of 69 dates, in which solar eclipses occur in a lapse of 33 years.

Today it is important to emphasize the deep respect that the Maya civilization had towards life and nature in general.

Who can predict what other great scientific conquests and developments these people could have achieved, if they had not been conquered in blood and fire, and subjected to an ethnocide that affected nearly 50 million people in the course of 500 years.

I would describe the meaning of this Nobel Prize, in the first place as a tribute to the indian people who have been sacrificed and have disappeared because they aimed at a more dignified and just life with fraternity and understanding among the human beings. To those who are no longer alive to keep up the hope for a change in the situation in respect of poverty and marginalization of the indians, of those who have been banished, of the helpless in Guatemala as well as in the entire American continent.

This growing concern is comforting, even though it comes 500 years later, to the suffering, the discrimination, the oppression and the exploitation that our people have been exposed to, but who, thanks to their own [vision of the cosmos] and concept of life, have managed to withstand and finally see some promising prospects. How those roots, that were to be eradicated, now begin to grow with strength, hopes and visions for the future!

The Original Rights of the People

It also represents a sign of the growing international interest for, and understanding of the original rights of the people, of the future of more than 60 million indians that live in our America, and their uproar because of the 500 years of oppression that they have endured. For the genocides beyond comparison that they have had to suffer all this time, and from which other countries and the elite of the Americas have profited and taken advantage.

Let there be freedom for the indians, wherever they may be in the American Continent or else in the world, because while they are alive, a glow of hope will be alive as well as the real concept of life.

The expressions of great happiness by the indian organizations in the entire continent and the worldwide congratulations received for the award of the Nobel Peace Prize, clearly indicate the great importance of this decision. It is the recognition of the European debt to the American indigenous people; it is an appeal to the conscience of humanity so that those conditions of marginalization that condemned them to colonialism and exploitation may be eradicated; it is a cry for life, peace, justice, equality and fraternity between human beings.

The peculiarities of the vision of the indian people are expressed according to the way in which they relate. First of all, between human being, through communication. Second, with the earth, as with our mother, because she gives us our lives and is not a mere merchandise. Third, with nature, because we are integral parts of it, and not its owners.

To us mother earth is not only a source of economic riches that give us the maize, which is our life, but she also provides so many other things that the privileged ones of today strive after. The earth is the root and the source of our culture. She keeps our memories, she receives our ancestors and she therefore demands that we honour her and return to her, with tenderness and respect, those goods that she gives us. We have to take care of her and look after mother earth so that our children and grandchildren may continue to benefit from her. If the world does not learn now to show respect to nature, what kind of future will the new generations have?

From these basic features derive behaviour, rights and obligations in the American Continent, for indians as well as for non-indians, whether they be racially mixed, blacks, whites or Asian. The whole society has the obligation to show mutual respect, to learn from each other and to share material and scientific achievements, in the most convenient way. The indians have never had, and they do not have, the place that they should have occupied in the progress and benefits of science and technology, although they have represented an important basis.

If the indian civilizations and the European civilizations could have made exchanges in a peaceful and harmonious manner, without destruction, exploitation, discrimination and poverty, they could, no doubt, have achieved greater and more valuable conquests for humanity.

Let us not forget that when the Europeans came to America, there were flourishing and strong civilizations there. One cannot talk about a discovery of America, because one discovers that which one does not know about, or that which is hidden. But America and its native civilizations had discovered themselves long before the fall of the Roman Empire and the Medieval Europe. The significance of its cultures form part of the heritage of humanity and continue to astonish the learned ones.

The Value of Cultural Identity

I think it is necessary that the indian people, of which I am a member, should contribute with its science and its knowledge to human development because we have enormous potentials and we could intercalate our very ancient heritage with the achievements of the civilization in Europe as well as in other parts of the world.

But this contribution, that to our understanding is a recovery of the natural and cultural heritage, must take place based on a rational and consensual plan in respect of the right to make use of knowledge and natural resources, with guarantees as to equality both towards government and society.

We the indians are willing to combine tradition with modernism, but not at all costs. We will not tolerate nor permit that our future be planned as possible guardians of ethno-touristic projects at continental level.

At a time when the commemoration of the Fifth Centenary of the arrival of Columbus in America has repercussions all over the world, the revival of hopes for the indian people claims that we reassert to the world our existence and the value of our cultural identity. It demands that we endeavour to actively participate in the decisions that concern our destiny, in the building-up of our countries/nations. Should we, in spite of all, not be taken into consideration? There are factors that guarantee our future: struggle and endurance; courage; the decision to maintain our traditions that have been exposed to so many perils and sufferings; solidarity towards our struggle on the part of numerous countries, governments, organizations and citizens of the world.

That is why I dream of the day when the relationship between the indigenous people and other people is strengthened; when they can join their potentialities and their capabilities and contribute to make life on this planet less unequal.

Today in the 47th period of sessions of the General Assembly, the United Nations (UN) will institute 1993 as the *International Year of the Indian People,* in the presence of well known chiefs of the organizations of the indian people and the Continental Resistance Movement of indians, blacks and other people. They will all formally participate in the opening of the working sessions in order to claim that 1993 be a year of specific actions to really place the indian people within their national contexts and the mutual international agreements.

The achievement of the *International Year of the Indian People* and the progress represented by the preparation of the project for the *Universal Declaration,* are the result of the participation of numerous indian brothers, non-governmental organizations and the successful efforts of the experts in the Working Group, in addition to the comprehensiveness shown by many countries in the United Nations.

We hope that the formulation of the project in respect of the *Declaration on the Rights of the Indian People* will examine and go deeply into the existing contradictions between the progress in terms of international rights and the difficult reality that we, the indo-Americans, experience in practice. . . .

An opinion is being formed everywhere about a phenomenon of today, that in spite of being expressed between wars and violence, calls upon the entire humanity to protect its historical values: unity in the diversity. And this calls upon us to reflect about the incorporation of important elements of change and transformation in all aspects of life on earth, in the search for specific and definite solutions to the deep ethical crisis that afflicts humanity. This will, no doubt, have decisive influence on the structuring of the future.

There is a possibility that some centers of political and economic power, some statesmen and intellectuals, have not yet managed to see the advantages of the active participation of the indian people in all the fields of human activity. However, the movement initiated by different political and intellectual "Amerindians" will finally convince them that, from an objective point of view, we are a constituent part of the historical alternatives that are being discussed at international levels.

Ladies and gentlemen, allow me to say some candid words about my country.

The attention that this Nobel Peace Prize has focused on Guatemala should imply that the violation of the human rights is no longer ignored internationally. It will also honour all those who have died struggling for social equality and justice in my country. . . .

As you know, I am myself a survivor of a massacred family.

The country collapsed into a crisis never seen before and the changes in the world forced and encouraged the military forces to permit a political opening that consisted in the preparation of a new Constitution, in an expansion of the political field and in the transfer of the government to civil sectors. We have had this new regime for eight years and in certain fields there have been some openings of importance.

However, in spite of these openings, repression and violation of human rights persist in the middle of an economic crisis that is becoming more and more acute, to the extent that 84% of the population is today considered as poor, and some 60% are considered as very poor. Impunity and terror continue to prevent people from freely expressing their needs and vital demands. The internal armed conflict still exists.

Human Rights Are at the Core

The political life in my country has lately circled around the search for a political solution to the global crisis and the armed conflict that has existed in Guatemala since 1962. This process was initiated by the agreement signed in this city of Oslo, between the Comisión Nacional de Reconciliación (National Commission for Reconciliation) with government mandate, and the Unidad Revolucionaria Nacional Guatemalteca-URNG-(The Guatemalan National Revolutionary Unity), as a necessary step to introduce to Guatemala the spirit of the Agreement of Esquipulas.

As a result of this agreement and conversations between the URNG and different sectors of the Guatemalan society, direct negotiations were initiated under the government of President Serrano, between the government and the guerrilla, as a result of which three agreements have already been signed. However, the subject of human rights has taken long time, because this subject constitutes the core in Guatemalan problematics, and around this core important differences have arisen. Nevertheless, there has been considerable progress.

The process of negotiations aims at reaching agreements in order to establish the basis for a real democracy in Guatemala and for the end of the war. As far as I understand, with the goodwill of the parties concerned and the active participation of the civil sectors, adapting to a great national unity, the phase of purposes and intentions could be left behind so that Guatemala could be pulled out of the crossroads that seems to become eternal.

Dialogues and the political negotiations are, no doubt, adequate means to solve these problems, in order to respond in a specific way to the vital and urgent needs for life and for the implementation of democracy for our Guatemalan people.

It is necessary to point out, here in Oslo, that the issue of the human rights in Guatemala constitutes just now the most urgent problem that has to be solved. My statement is neither incidental nor unjustified.

As has been ascertained by international institutions, such as the United Nations Commission of the Human Rights, the Interamerican Commission of the Human Rights and many other humanitarian organizations, Guatemala is one of the countries in America with the largest number of violations of these rights, the largest number of cases of impunity where security forces are generally involved. It is imperative that the repression and persecution of the people and the indians be stopped. The compulsory mobilization and integration of young people into the Patrols of Civil Self-defense, which to a great extent affects the indian people, must also be stopped.

Democracy in Guatemala must be built-up as soon as at all possible. It is necessary that the human rights be fully complied with, i.e.: put an end to racism; guarantee freedom to organize and to move within all sectors of the country. In short, it is imperative to open the fields to the multiethnic civil society with all its rights, to demilitarize the country and establish the basis for its development, so that it can be pulled out of today's underdevelopment and poverty.

Refugees

Among the most bitter dramas that a great percentage of the population has to endure, is the forced exodus. Which means, to be forced by military units and persecution to abandon their villages, their mother earth, where their ancestors rest, their environment, the nature that gave them life and the growth of their communities, all of which constitute a coherent system of social organization and functional democracy.

The case of the displaced and refugees in Guatemala is heartbreaking; some of them are condemned to live in exile in other countries, but the great majority live in exile in their own country. They are forced to wander from place to place, to live in ravines and inhospitable places, some not recognized as Guatemalan citizens, but all of them are condemned to poverty and hunger. There cannot be a real democracy as long as this problem is not satisfactorily solved and these people are reintegrated to their lands and villages.

In the new Guatemalan society there must be a fundamental reorganization in the matter of land possession, to allow for the development of the agricultural potentials, as well as for the return to the legitimate owners of the land that was taken away from them. And not to forget that this process of reorganization must be carried out with the greatest respect towards nature, in order to protect her and return to her, her strength and capability to generate life.

No less characteristic in a democracy is social justice. This demands a solution to the frightening indexes of infantile mortality, of malnutrition, lack of education, . . . wages not sufficient to sustain life. These problems have a growing and painful impact on the Guatemalan population and there are no prospects and no hopes.

Among the features that characterize society today is the role of the woman, although woman emancipation has not been fully achieved so far by any country in the world.

The historical development in Guatemala reflects now the need and the irreversibility of the active contribution of the woman in the configuration of the new Guatemalan social order, of which, I humbly believe, the indian women already are a clear testimony. This Nobel Prize is a recognition to those who have been, and still are in most parts of the world, the most exploited of the exploited ones; the most discriminated of the discriminated ones, the most marginalized of the marginalized ones, but still they are the ones that produce life and riches.

Democracy, development and modernization of a country are impossible and incongruous without the solution of these problems.

In Guatemala it is just as important to recognize the identity and the rights of the indigenous people, that have been ignored and despised not only during the colonial period, but also in the republican one. It is not possible to conceive a democratic Guatemala, free and independent, without the indigenous identity shaping its character into all aspects of national existence.

It will undoubtedly be something new, a completely new experience, with features that, at the moment, we cannot describe. But it will authentically respond to history and the characteristics of the real Guatemalan nationality. The real profile that has been distorted for such a long time.

This urgency and this vital need are the issues that urge me, at this moment, from this rostrum, to ask the national opinion and the international community to show a more active interest in Guatemala.

The Need for Peace

Taking into consideration that in connection with my role as a Nobel Prize winner, in the process of negotiations for peace in Guatemala many possibilities have been handled, but now I think that this role is more likely to be the role of a promoter of peace, of national unity, for protection of the rights of the indigenous people. In such a way that I may take initiatives in accordance with those arising, and thereby prevent the Peace

Prize from becoming a piece of paper that has been filed.

I call upon all the social and ethnic sectors that constitute the people of Guatemala to participate actively in the efforts to find a peaceful solution to the armed conflict, to build up a sound unity between the "ladinos" (of indian and Spanish descent), the blacks and the indians, all of whom must create within their diversity, the guatemality.

Along these same lines, I invite the international community to contribute with specific actions so that the parties involved may overcome the differences that at this stage keep negotiations in a wait-and-see state, and thereby succeed, first of all, in signing an agreement on human rights. And then, re-initiate the rounds of negotiation and find those issues on which to compromise, allowing for the peace agreement to be signed and immediately verified, because I have no doubt that this will bring about a great relief to the prevailing situation in Guatemala.

Ladies and gentlemen, the fact that I have given preference to the American continent, and in particular to my country, does not mean that I do not have an important place in my mind and in my heart for the concern of other people of the world and their constant struggle for the defense of peace, of the rights to a life and all its inalienable rights. The majority of us who are gathered here today constitute an example of the above, and along these lines I would humbly extend to you my gratitude.

Many things have changed in these last years. There have been great changes of world-wide character. The East-West confrontation has ceased to exist and the cold war has come to an end. These changes, which exact forms cannot yet be predicted, have left gaps that the people of the world have known how to make use in order to come forward, struggle and win national terrain and international recognition.

Today we must fight for a better world, without poverty, without racism, with peace in the Middle East and in South-East Asia, to where I address a plea for the liberation of Mrs. Aung San Suu Kyi, winner of the Nobel Peace Prize 1991; for a just and peaceful solution of the Balkans; for the end of the Apartheid in the South of Africa; for the stability in Nicaragua; that the peace agreement in El Salvador be observed; for the re-establishment of democracy in Haiti; for the complete sovereignty of Panama; because all of that constitutes the highest aims as to justice, in the international situation.

A world at peace that could provide consistency, interrelation and concordance in respect of the economic, social and cultural structures of the societies. That could have deep roots and sound influence.

We have in our mind the deepest felt demands of the entire humanity when we strive for a peaceful coexistence and the preservation of the environment.

The struggle we fight purifies and shapes the future.

Our history is a live history that has throbbed, withstood and survived many centuries of sacrifice. Now it comes forward again with strength. The seeds, dormant for such a long time, break out today with some uncertainty, although they germinate in a world that is at present characterized by confusion and vagueness.

There is no doubt that this process will be long and complex, but it is no Utopia and we, the indians, we have now confidence in its implementation.

The people of Guatemala will mobilize and will be aware of its strength to build up a worthy future. It is preparing itself to sow the future, to free itself from atavisms, to rediscover itself. To build up a country with a genuine national identity. To start a new life.

By combining all the shades and nuances of the "ladinos", the "garífunas" and indians in the Guatemalan ethnic mosaic, we must interlace a number of colours without arising contradictions, without they becoming grotesque nor antagonistic, but we must give them brightness and a superior quality, just the way our weavers weave. A typical "güipil" shirt brilliantly composed, a gift to humanity.

Globalization and Human Rights

Pierre Sané

Born in Senegal and educated in France in business and economics, Pierre Sané has been engaged in various levels of development work during his career. He worked for the International Development Research Center, a Canadian international organization dedicated to helping developing countries build their scientific and industrial capabilities. In 1992, Amnesty International, a human rights organization, appointed him as its secretary general. Founded in 1961, the goal of Amnesty International is to realize all the principles of the Universal Declaration of Human Rights (UDHR). The organization began with focusing on prisoners of conscience—people detained for the ideas or beliefs that differ from governments in control. That work has expanded along with the rest of the human rights movement to include the rights of refugees, abolition of the death penalty, women's rights, socially responsible economics, and other issues.

Sané gave the following speech to the Energy Conference 2000, in Sanderstolen, Norway. The Energy Policy Foundation of Norway has sponsored this annual energy conference for over twenty-five years. It is considered by many leaders to be the most important informal meeting for policy and decision makers in the oil and gas industry. Topics focus on international energy policy issues and their impact on global economic health and politics.

Sané's speech addresses why it is important for businesses to take responsibility for human rights issues. He points out that improved human rights records strengthen

From Pierre Sané's speech to the Energy Conference in Norway, February 2, 2000. Copyright © 2000 Amnesty International, One Easton St., London WC1X 0DW, United Kingdom; www.amnesty.org.

political stability, which in turn protects investments and economic productivity. Emphasizing that the enormous power and influence multinational corporations wield must be handled responsibly, he proposes a code of conduct requiring companies to ask about a country's human rights record before investing there.

L et me first extend my thanks, on behalf of Amnesty International (AI), to the Energy Policy Foundation for this invitation and opportunity to exchange with the leaders of the oil and gas industry. On this occasion I am joined by my colleagues Jan Borgen, SG of AI Norway and Salil Tripathi, International Coordinator for our work on economic relations and human rights.

AI is a 40-year-old democratic movement with one million members in 160 countries. Its objectives are to promote observance of human rights everywhere and to oppose specific violations of international human rights law such as wrongful political imprisonment, unfair trials, torture and ill-treatment, judicial and extra-judicial executions, disappearances—to promote the respect of humanitarian principles in armed conflicts and the rights of refugees and asylum seekers. In so doing we seek to engage governments, individuals and all organs of society to take action whenever appropriate to promote the goals of the UDHR [Universal Declaration of Human Rights], that is a world free from fear and free from want.

And business of course has a role to play. Let's look briefly at the odds first:

The 20th century has been the bloodiest in recorded human history. Between world wars, genocide, colonial wars, man-made famines, ethnic cleansing, massive human rights violations, close to 200 million people have died at the hands of governments, warlords and economic decision makers.

The 21st century is fraught with dangers: growing poverty and inequality everywhere, proliferation of weapons of mass destruction (from nuclear weapons to small weapons), roll back the limits of barbarism, persistence of racism and discrimination.

But the 21st century is also full of promises: A fully developed set of international human rights treaties and standards; a growing, dynamic human rights movement the world over engaged in education, monitoring and campaigning for human rights. Hopefully soon an ICC [International Criminal Court] where perpetrators of crimes against humanity and war crimes will be tried. If we want to protect future generations action is required.

The Responsibility of Business

If governments are still the primary bodies accountable for upholding human rights everywhere the responsibility of the business community is inescapable.

But why should business care about human rights? After all, its chief mission, many would agree, is to create wealth and generate profits for its shareholders.

I can point to five reasons why business should care about human rights.

1. The first one is the moral argument. We do not need to convince managers and boardrooms that the amputation of children's limbs in Sierra Leone in order to terrorize a population and win a war is wrong, or that the gang rape of women by Serb soldiers in Kosovo is evil, or that the killing of civilians in East Timor or Chechnya is to be condemned. These acts are wrong, insidious. They have been prohibited internationally.

2. The second argument is the legitimacy of human rights. They have been codified in treaties ratified by governments. Peoples the world over are struggling to hold their governments accountable for the implementation of international law. Believe me, if a free ballot was upheld globally today, overwhelmingly people will say they want their human rights, all their human rights.

3. The third argument is that it is in the interest of business to see human rights protected. The rule of law protects investments by guaranteeing political stability. An educated and healthy population increases economic productivity. A company tarnished by controversies around human rights violations can see its reputation destroyed and its profitability threatened.

4. Fourthly, companies and more specifically, Multinational Corporations have secured for themselves freedoms to operate, which has given them enormous power to affect the lives of people; with power comes responsibility.

5. Finally, the Universal Declaration of Human Rights (UDHR) calls upon all organs of society to protect and promote human rights. The ILO [International Labour Organization] conventions protect the rights of the workers. Other conventions place direct responsibility on companies to act in accordance with international human rights law.

Courses of Action

How then to turn concern into action? And what is it that business can do to protect and promote human rights everywhere?

Let me suggest five courses of action.

1. First business needs to debunk a few myths and stop hiding behind the spurious arguments put forth by some governments such as:

Cultural relativism. In other words, "our people have different values. You cannot impose on human rights which are a western construct." Your response as pointed out by Kofi Annan [secretary-general of the United Nations], should be that humanity is indivisible and human rights are as African as they are Asian or European. Mind you, those governments would have in the same breath adopted communism or capitalism which as we know emerged from the banks of the river Thames.

Another myth is *economic determinism.* That is, economic growth will lead to the development of a middle class who in turn will demand civil and political rights. Your response, as agreed by the world community in Vienna six years ago, should be: Human Rights are Indivisible.

The third myth is that *human rights action is political and business should not interfere in domestic politics.* If that is so then business should not interfere to change legislation pertaining to repatriation of profits or labour laws or environmental protection. The truth is that human rights are a matter of international law and the law must be upheld. It is a perfectly legitimate demand.

2. The second course of action is to develop codes of conduct which are consistent with international standards. To ensure that they are implemented, including by subcontractors. To allow independent monitoring and public reporting.

3. The third course of action for business is to lobby governments to adjust their legislation, develop the mechanisms and institutions at home and abroad to ensure that human rights will be protected. Working for an effective justice system to protect commercial agreements is not enough. All agreements, including human rights treaties, must be safeguarded.

4. Business must enter into dialogue with governments, NGOs [nongovernmental organizations], trade unions and with other businesses to continuously define and refine roles and strategies.

5. Finally, the rights of the workers and of the communities directly affected by business operations must be safeguarded.

The Role of Oil Companies

Turning now to the oil industry I believe it has a unique role to play:

Oil is unique in the critical role it plays in the functioning of the world economy. Oil companies are present everywhere for purposes of extraction, refinement, transportation and distribution.

Oil explorers very often go to dangerous places with weak legal infrastructure, emerging democracies, in countries ravaged by conflicts and wars; where to go being dictated by geology, the issue is rather in what way.

In many producing countries the oil revenue will represent the lion-share of the government's revenue. This combined with a lack of democratic accountability makes political competition fierce and at times violent.

As the oil industry expands and explores new fields, develops new mandates, builds new pipelines and refineries it finds itself in the midst of strife, unrest and conflicts in countries where international human rights law is violated daily.

1. In such an environment it is particularly important for the industry to develop its own set of principles and guidelines in order to ensure ethical behavior and in order to meet

expectations of consumers—in markets at home and of employees globally. These codes of conduct must be based on international standards and the latter must prevail when domestic legislation encompasses "bad" laws, that is laws which are in clear breach of internationally agreed standards.

2. These codes will require the constant attention of top management, the training and awareness raising of all staff. For example, Texas Instruments has a simple ethics test printed on a business card and given to every employee with the expectation that the employee will carry it in his or her wallet.

Is the action legal?

Does it comply with our values?

If you do it, will you feel bad?

How will it look in the newspapers?

If you know it's wrong, don't do it.

If you're not sure, ask.

Keep asking until you get an answer.

3. Companies should also require the same standard of behavior from [their] suppliers, contractors and business associates. The human rights text should be added to the criteria companies usually apply to select suppliers and contractors, such as quality of product, cost, punctuality, standards, and so on.

4. Implementing the codes will of course require good understanding of the challenges and opportunities in each country. For example, Mr. Tor Ivar Pedersen, the president of Statoil Azerbaijan, said in December [1999] in Oslo that human rights should be a natural part of a company's activities as is now the case with health, safety and the environment. "Human rights," he said, "could easily be one of the considerations taken in parallel to the full assessment" before investing in a particular country. This is the way to plan ahead, to anticipate human rights challenges, and to find ways to ensure that investments and operations will have a positive impact on society.

5. The codes of conduct should be seen as work in progress continually monitored and improved through constant dialogues with the UN [United Nations] bodies, NGOs, local communities, governments.

Let me repeat: what the oil industry decides has importance far beyond the industry. It can set standards for other industries. It can help enormously in making this planet a better place for all. At a more immediate level it can ensure that a company is not caught in the eye of a human rights storm.

What Does Responsibility Mean?

There is the view that human rights are, somehow, the responsibility of the government, not of companies. But I have a few simple questions:

When a company like Mobil innocently assists in building premises for an army in a country like Indonesia and that army then uses the premises to torture members of an armed opposition group, can the company shun responsibility?

When a company like BP-Amoco deals with a private security firm and does not scrutinize its links with sections of the army involved in human rights violations in a strife-torn country like Colombia, can the company say it is not responsible?

When a company like Shell partners a state-run monopoly in a developing country like Nigeria, where revenue-sharing within provinces perpetuates economic inequities, and these inequities lead to armed conflict between groups of the population, can the company step aside saying it has no role?

When a company like Chevron calls in local police authorities in Nigeria to break up a demonstration on its premises to protect its property and staff, both worthy priorities, and if the local police authorities use disproportionate force, shouldn't the company require the security forces to use the UN's Basic Principles on the Use of Force and Firearms and the UN Code of Conduct for Law Enforcement Officials? These minimum standards are highlighted by the UN Global Compact for business, spearheaded by Secretary-General Kofi Annan, and to which many large companies subscribe.

When a company like Total is operating in an area of Burma where independent reports from other sites suggest that forced labour is used to work on government projects, can the company say it is a guest in Burma, and therefore its hands are tied?

All these examples are known to you, and you have to

grapple with such issues regularly. While corporations are not directly responsible for all human rights violations committed by the states in which they operate, they are in a position to ensure that they are not complicit in those violations and that they use their legitimate influence over the host government to promote and protect human rights.

How can the industry get there? We believe companies do not have to wait for government initiatives—the body of international protocols, treaties, covenants and conventions that can help a company write its code of conduct exists. In fact there is a mechanism that can assure compliance.

For much of the early part of this century, the oil industry was known for the so-called seven sisters which controlled the exploration, production, refining, transportation and distribution of this commodity. That powerful oligopoly was challenged in 1973 by the Organization of Petroleum Exporting Countries, or OPEC, which dramatically decided to come together and raise the price of crude oil. This affected the whole global economy. But it also led to new discoveries, of energy-saving technologies, of exploration of alternative sources of energy.

In our discussions with multinational corporations, we have found that most companies have common goals: they want to invest in countries which respect the rule of law, which guarantee equality before law, which have transparent laws, which believe in good governance, which seek to improve the lot of their people, and which respect the human rights of the population. Yet, that collective goal disintegrates at individual levels in some cases.

When we ask why, the companies say this is because all companies will not act in concert. A French company will say, if we don't do it somebody else will. An American company will say if we don't play along the Europeans will.

I suggest that senior executives of the oil industry come together and deliberate on this issue. I urge that they make public the minimum standards they require from countries, from the police force of the governments, and from the international community, so that human rights are protected and in turn make public their own commitment.

This is not as outlandish as it might appear. We are in

Norway, but a hundred years have passed since Ibsen wrote *The Enemy of the People*. Those who seek positive change will not be hounded the way Dr. Thomas Stockmann was!

After all, companies from disparate industries come together to lobby for trade liberalization at the World Trade Organisation. A wide cross-section of industries come together to seek a multilateral agreement on investments at the Organisation of Economic Cooperation and Development. Companies have common concerns on capital repatriation, on free movement of goods, services and currencies. Why not demand protection of human rights? Why not make respect of human rights, of the rule of law, of good governance and transparency, of freedom for the people, as essential an element of the new architecture of globalization, as the free movement of capital, currencies, and commodities? Why can't the agents of globalization be the agents of the globalization of human rights?

Human Trafficking and the Global Sex Industry: A Human Rights Framework

Mary Robinson

Born in Ireland at the end of World War II, Mary Robinson nearly epitomizes the changes that have taken place for women and Ireland in the past fifty years. She has two law degrees, served the Labor Party in the Irish Parliament for twenty years, and in 1990 became the first woman president of Ireland. She left that position a few months shy of her term in 1997 upon her appointment as the United Nations High Commissioner for Human Rights. Only the second person to hold this position, she was appointed by the UN Secretary-General Kofi Annan with the intent to bring greater visibility to the position and to show the importance of human rights issues on the agenda of the United Nations and its agencies. Robinson, known for her outspoken nature, brings a keen awareness of human rights action to the political table.

In the following speech, Robinson addresses the international problem of human trafficking. Economic conditions are so poor in many countries that people both willingly and unwittingly place themselves in positions where they can become literal slaves in other countries or enclaves. For example, women and girls are often forced into prostitution. Robinson contends that any solution to this problem must focus primarily on the human rights of the victims.

From Mary Robinson's speech delivered to a Non-Governmental Organization/ International Governmental Organization Consultation on trafficking in Geneva, Switzerland, June 21, 1999.

Everywhere I travel I see evidence of the growing problem of trafficking and its links to the global sex industry. Invariably, the picture presented by the victims of trafficking is of money being made at the expense of human dignity and freedom. During a visit to Cambodia in January 1998 I heard first-hand accounts of the brutality inflicted on women and girls who had been trafficked into prostitution. When I went to the Former Republic of Yugoslavia and neighbouring States in May of this year [1999] I found that the growing problem of trafficking was adding to the miseries of the refugee population in that part of the world. I have just returned from Russia where I heard stories of huge numbers of Russian and Ukrainian women being tricked or coerced into situations of danger and exploitation. Poverty, inequality and discrimination seem to be the unifying factors in each of these sad situations.

The sheer scope of the worldwide trade in human beings and the misery it generates can appear overwhelming. In the face of such odds, I am encouraged by the energy and determination that I have witnessed in the nongovernmental community. That is what struck me while visiting the makeshift women's shelter in Cambodia. It is largely thanks to the nongovernmental community—particularly those working so tirelessly in the field—that trafficking is on the international political agenda. We must continue the fight in order to ensure that this attention results in the kind of policy and attitudinal changes that are so necessary.

While congratulating ourselves on certain successes we must remain aware of the fact that ideological and conceptual differences have prevented significant progress. I refer in particular to the debate over prostitution which has both energized and polarized the anti-trafficking community. We must accept the fact that opinions will differ on certain key issues. Differences of opinion are to be expected and can even be a positive force. Such differences should not, however, be allowed to take over. The resulting paralysis does a great disservice to the women, children and men who most need our help. I encourage all those engaged in the fight against trafficking to identify the many commonalities that should allow us all to work productively together.

My own position and that of my Office is based on two fundamental principles:

—First: that human rights must be at the core of any credible anti-trafficking strategy; and

—Second: that we must work from the perspective of those who most need their human rights protected and promoted.

These two principles are, of course, interrelated. By placing human rights at the centre of our analysis, we are forced to consider the needs of the trafficked person—and thereby to confront the poverty, inequality and discrimination which is at the root of this phenomenon. What does it mean to make human rights the core of our anti-trafficking work? For me it means first and foremost, acknowledging that trafficking and related practices such as debt bondage and forced prostitution and false marriage are themselves a violation of the basic human rights to which all persons are entitled. The right to life; the right to dignity and security; the right to just and favourable conditions of work; the right to health; the right to be recognized as a person before the law. These are rights which we all possess—irrespective of our sex, our nationality, our social status, our occupation or any other difference.

A human rights approach also demands that we acknowledge the responsibility of governments to protect and promote the rights of all persons within their jurisdiction. This responsibility translates into a legal obligation on governments to work towards eliminating trafficking and related exploitation. Passivity and inaction are insufficient. Tolerance or complicity are inexcusable.

Finally, for me, as High Commissioner, a human rights approach to trafficking means that all parts of the United Nations, not just my Office, should integrate human rights into their analysis of the problem and into their responses. This is the only way to retain a focus on the trafficked person: to ensure that trafficking is not simply reduced to a problem of migration, a problem of public order; or a problem of organized crime.

That brings me to the work of my Office. Very soon after my appointment I decided that trafficking must become a priority area of our work. The recent allocation of financial and human resources has enabled me to set up a modest

Anti-Trafficking Programme. The basic objective of the Programme is to work towards the integration of human rights into international, regional and national anti-trafficking initiatives. Our emphasis is on legal and policy development. We do not aim to undertake large-scale projects or to otherwise duplicate the excellent initiatives that are being undertaken elsewhere. Instead, as far as possible, we try to act as a catalyst and a support for the work of others. In the following paragraphs I will give some examples of our work.

At the international level my Office has been closely following the development of two important Protocols to the draft Convention against Transnational Organized Crime. One of these protocols concerns illegal migration. The other deals with trafficking of persons. We have analysed both draft instruments from a human rights perspective and submitted this analysis—together with specific recommendations to the Ad-Hoc Working Group responsible for the drafting process. I need not remind those working in the trafficking field that this process represents the first legislative consideration of the trafficking issue in over half a century. It is very important to ensure that the end result represents a step forward in eliminating trafficking and securing the rights of trafficked persons. At a very minimum we must ensure that there is no retreat from earlier legal commitments.

It is equally important for us to make the link between illegal migration on the one hand, and trafficking in persons on the other. These are rightly being considered as two separate issues. However, the crossover potential is enormous. Today's illegal migrant may well be yesterday's—or tomorrow's—trafficking victim. Both situations present a grave threat to the protection of human rights and both therefore deserve our closest attention.

My Office is increasingly directing its anti-trafficking activities to the regional and sub-regional levels. In Central and Eastern Europe we are cooperating with the Council of Europe and IOM [International Office of Migration] on a project which initially targeted refugees from Kosovo and is now more broadly focused on trafficking trouble-spots of Central and Southern Europe. Our Office in Sarajevo is also undertaking significant preventive and assistance work throughout the territory of the Former Yugoslavia.

In the Asian region our attention is focusing on the draft Convention on Trafficking in Women and Girls which is being elaborated under the auspices of the South Asian Association for Regional Cooperation. My concerns here are identical to those I expressed earlier in connection with the Vienna Protocols. The SAARC Governments are to be congratulated for taking up this complex and problematic issue. At the same time it is essential that all efforts be made to ensure that the end result represents an advance for trafficked persons and their human rights.

In Nepal, my Office is currently developing a project, along with the local UNDP [United Nations Development Programme] Office, that will pilot a rights-based approach to the trafficking problem. The pilot will initially be implemented in two districts in Nepal. We are relying very heavily on the local NGO [non-governmental organization] community to ensure the success of this important endeavour. Other activities in Asia include a dialogue between my office and ASEAN [Association of South East Asian Nations] States on the issue of trafficking and transnational organized crime. We are also working closely with the National Human Rights Commissions of the Asia-Pacific region in order to assist them in taking up the issue of trafficking.

Finally, but importantly, recent and significant contributions to the UN Trust Fund on Contemporary Forms of Slavery have enabled us to provide a number of travel and project grants to NGOs working on behalf of victims of trafficking.

We all agree on the enormity of the problem at hand and on the difficulty of developing credible solutions. We should not allow differences of emphasis to turn into divisions that prevent us from realizing our common goal—to stand up for the rights of victims of trafficking wherever and whoever they are. We will only succeed if we harness our collective endeavours. I urge you to work together in a constructive, cooperative spirit. I urge you to take up the tools of human rights in your fight against trafficking and to focus on the needs of trafficked persons. That is the way forward and I am proud to be part of this journey.

Appendix of Biographies

Susan B. Anthony

Susan B. Anthony was born in 1820 in Massachusetts. She worked as a teacher from the age of seventeen to twenty-nine, when she took over running her father's farm in New York. At this time, she began to give lectures on women's rights and developed friendships with abolitionist leaders such as Frederick Douglass and Amy Post. She met Elizabeth Cady Stanton in 1851, and together they formed the Women's New York State Temperance Society, an organization that championed the right of women to vote on the issue of temperance and to divorce alcoholic husbands. Anthony and Stanton also advocated for equal educational opportunities for women, less restrictive forms of clothing for women, property rights for married women, and more liberal divorce laws.

During the Civil War Anthony shifted her focus to the cause of abolition, promoting a constitutional amendment to abolish slavery. After the war, she and Stanton advocated a constitutional amendment guaranteeing the voting rights of all citizens. They established the National Woman Suffrage Association in 1869 with the goal of establishing women's right to vote.

Anthony and several other women cast ballots in the presidential election of 1872. She was arrested, convicted, and fined for this violation of the law. She refused to pay the fine and spoke persuasively of the injustice of her arrest. This event increased support for a constitutional amendment for women's suffrage. Although this amendment was defeated in 1876, Anthony continued her efforts. She died in 1906, fourteen years before suffrage was secured by the Nineteenth Amendment.

John Ball

John Ball's early life remains a mystery. He was ordained as a peasant priest, but the date of this event is unknown. It is thought that he was a priest at York, then moved to the south of England. In Essex, in 1366, the church banned him from preaching. Several sermons have been attributed to Ball that reflect a priest who preached against social inequality and the excesses of the church. Eventually, in 1376, he was excommunicated for preaching against the pope.

During the 1380s Ball was imprisoned in Maidstone for continuing to speak out against the corruption of the clergy and the church. Freed from that prison by the peasant uprising of 1381, Ball gave sermons at Blackheath (near Greenwich on the south bank of the Thames), where the rebels gathered before entering London. On July 13, 1381, some weeks after the uprising was suppressed, the king's men captured Ball in St. Albans, where they sentenced him to death. He was hanged, drawn, and quartered.

John Brown

Born in Connecticut in 1800, John Brown became one of the most renowned militant white American abolitionists. He supported his family by working as a tanner, sheep drover, wool merchant, and farmer. He traveled through many states—including Ohio, Pennsylvania, Kansas, and New York—fighting against slavery.

In October 1859 he led an armed band of sixteen whites and five blacks in a raid on the federal armory at Harpers Ferry on the Potomac River. He was captured and tried for murder, slave insurrection, and treason against the state. After his conviction, he was hanged and immediately became a martyr for the abolitionists and many other radical activists.

Frederick Douglass

Frederick Douglass and his mother, Harriet Bailey, were slaves of Captain Aaron Anthony. Anthony, who may have been Douglass's father, owned about thirty slaves and three farms. Douglass was separated from his mother as an infant and was raised by his maternal grandmother. Determined to receive an education, the first book he bought was *The Columbian Orator*, a standard rhetoric text that contained famous speeches on human freedom. While running errands, he would exchange food with poor, hungry white children for reading lessons. The fact that a book of speeches was the first book read by Douglass proved prophetic and helps to explain, at least to a limited degree, his eventual success and gift as an orator.

In 1848 Douglass was the only man in attendance at the first women's convention at Seneca Falls, New York, to endorse Elizabeth Cady Stanton's female suffrage resolution. Douglass stood consistently at the hub of the leading political activities of the day, although in 1851 he broke his relations with the renowned abolitionist William Lloyd Garrison over Garrison's condemnation of the U.S. Constitution.

Douglass met and conferred with President Abraham Lincoln many times. After the Civil War Douglass received three appointments from three U.S. presidents. In 1889 President Benjamin Harrison appointed him minister to Haiti and chargé d'affaires to Santo Domingo.

On February 25, 1895, Douglass died of a heart attack on his estate, having just returned from attending a women's rights convention.

Mohandas K. Gandhi

Mohandas Karamchand Gandhi, an Indian born in 1869 in British-occupied India, led his country to independence. He began his adult life by studying law in England and eventually practiced in India and South Africa. Having experienced racial discrimination in England as well as in South Africa, in 1893 he decided to fight racial prejudice toward Indians in South Africa. During this time he began to read the Bible, Ralph Waldo Emerson, and Henry David Thoreau. His personal philosophy went through many changes, and in 1906 he openly abandoned his interest in worldly goods and Western ways and took a vow of celibacy for life. At this same time he announced the need for "home rule" in India.

He continued to live in South Africa and organized his first satyagraha (holding to the truth), a nonviolent, civil disobedience campaign held in response to what he saw as unjust discrimination laws. Eventually, in 1914, he secured an agreement from the South African government that promised the lifting of anti-Indian discrimination.

In 1915 Gandhi returned to India with a popularity unrivaled by other Indian leaders of the time. The Amritsar massacre of 1919, in which nearly four hundred Indian protesters were killed by British soldiers, provoked Indian nationalist consciousness, and Gandhi began to organize several satyagraha campaigns. Gandhi initiated a nonviolent, noncooperation movement, which officially lasted from September 1920 until February 1922 and included the following actions: resignation of titles by Indians; a boycott of government educational institutions, the courts, government service, foreign goods, and elections; and the eventual refusal to pay taxes. In September 1920 Gandhi assumed leadership of the Indian National Congress in Calcutta. The stage seemed to be firmly set for Gandhi's influence on India's independent future.

Arrested for sedition in 1922, Gandhi served two years of a six-year prison sentence. After his release, Gandhi participated less in politics, and, for the first time in his life, he traveled to the Indian countryside. Moved by the level of poverty that most people in India endured, he began to live a simpler life himself, spinning his own loincloth and eventually choosing to wear the white dhoti, the characteristic clothing of the Indian lower classes. In 1930, in protest to an imposed British tax on salt, a move that deeply affected the poorest of Indians, once again Gandhi launched a satyagraha campaign. Gandhi was arrested, but he wielded an influence that the British government could not ignore. Throughout his life Gandhi often exercised as much power from within prison as from without.

As the move toward Indian independence grew, Gandhi strongly opposed Britain's partition of India into two states: a Muslim state, which would become Pakistan; and the Hindu state of India. However, other Indian leaders accepted the partition plan, and in 1947 the Independence of India Bill was passed. Although Gandhi hailed August 15, 1947, as a day of celebration for Indian independence, he deplored the division of the country and soon began to fast for communal peace. In January 1948 he ended his six-day fast after he was assured of communal harmony between Muslims and Hindus. Two weeks later, on January 30, 1948, as a result of his desire to circumvent the establishment of two nations, Gandhi was assassinated while on his way to evening prayers.

Tenzin Gyatso, Fourteenth Dalai Lama of Tibet

Tenzin Gyatso was born in China to Tibetan parents in 1935. Considered to be the incarnation of Bodhisattva Avalokiteshvara, he became the fourteenth Dalai Lama—the spiritual and political leader of Tibet—in 1940, at the age of five. In 1950 the Chinese invaded Tibet and began to take over rule of the country. In 1959 the Tibetans revolted against Chinese rule. After a bloody confrontation, the revolt was suppressed, and the Dalai Lama fled to exile in India, where he has lived since that time.

Since 1959 the Chinese have systematically dismantled Tibetan culture. While in exile, the Dalai Lama has continued to fulfill the role of spiritual leader of Tibet, speaking out for the liberation of his country from Chinese occupation, calling for the protection of human rights and religious freedom in Tibet, and expressing his vision of world peace. He received the Nobel Peace Prize in 1989.

Patrick Henry

Born in Virginia in 1736, Patrick Henry failed in his early efforts in business. However, as a lawyer his fortunes changed. In 1763, at age twenty-seven, he became renowned as a brilliant orator in the *Parson's Cause* case. Parsons of the Church of England attempted to tax colonists who believed in other religions. Henry fought against the imposition of this tax and triumphed in his efforts. The people carried him out of the courtroom in triumph.

Two years later he gained his first seat in the House of Burgesses in Williamsburg, Virginia, and gave a speech that challenged the legitimacy of the Stamp Act imposed by England. He defied King George III with the words, "If this be treason, make the most of it." Ten years later, during the Second Virginia Convention at St. John's Church in Richmond, he gave the speech that has become oft-quoted as the catalyst for the colonies' ultimate cry for revolution, saying, "Give me liberty or give me death."

Henry continued his leadership after the Revolution as the first elected governor of Virginia and with his efforts toward the adoption of the Bill of Rights. He was determined that the establishment of the new government include protection of basic civil liberties.

In 1794 Henry retired to his seven-hundred-acre estate at Red Hill and became one of the one hundred wealthiest landowners in Virginia. He continued to try civil and criminal cases as a lawyer, but he repeatedly refused offers from President George Washington to serve in public office. He declined offers to serve as secretary of state, chief justice of the Supreme Court, and governor in the general. He also refused an offer from President John Adams to serve on the mission to France.

In 1799 Henry gave his last public oration. Washington had persuaded him to become a candidate for the state legislature, and he was elected to the House of Delegates. The unity of the young nation was in danger due to individual states' nullifying acts of the federal government. It was an inspirational and nonpartisan appeal for unity to preserve the country. Three months later, on June 6, 1799, Patrick Henry died. The historian Henry Adams reported that nothing in Henry's life was more noble than this last public speech.

John Paul II

Pope John Paul II, born Karol Wojtyla in Poland in 1920, became the first non-Italian pope of the Catholic Church since 1523 and the first ever Polish pope. He taught ethics at universities in Kraków and Lublin and published works on theological and philosophical topics as well as poetry and a play. He was consecrated as a bishop in 1958, became archbishop of Kraków in 1964, and became a cardinal in 1967.

As pope, John Paul II has continued to implement the decisions of Vatican II and places special emphasis on devotion to the Virgin Mary. He has traveled widely, increasing the international visibility of the papacy. Despite the physical setback caused when he was shot in St. Peter's Square on May 13, 1981, by a Turkish terrorist, during his pontificate he has visited over fifty countries. John Paul continues to travel widely despite his increasing age and frailty. In 1998 he visited Cuba; in 1999 he visited Romania and Georgia, becoming the first pope to visit predominantly Orthodox countries; in 2000 he visited the Holy Land; and in 2001 he retraced St. Paul's missionary journeys in Greece, Syria, and Malta.

Martin Luther King Jr.

In 1955, while completing his Ph.D. from Boston University, Martin Luther King Jr. decided to return to the South and become pastor of the Dexter Avenue Baptist Church in Montgomery, Alabama. At that time Rosa Parks had refused to obey the city's segregation rules, which prohibited black residents from riding in the front of a bus. During the ensuing bus boycott, King was elected president of the newly established Montgomery Improvement Association. King's exceptional oratorical skills and his strong personal leadership style were quickly recognized. His life was threatened with bombs and he was convicted with others on charges of interfering with the bus company's operations. Nonetheless, Montgomery's buses were desegregated in December 1956, after the U.S. Supreme Court declared that Alabama's segregation laws were unconstitutional.

Building on the success of the bus boycott, King and others organized the Southern Christian Leadership Conference (SCLC), first in the South and later throughout the country. Inspired by Gandhi, King became known for the nonviolent resistance tactics that he employed in the pursuit of black voting rights and improved civil liberties.

As a preacher, King frequently spoke of the importance of ecumenism and the need to transcend race, class, and nationalism. He said on December 24, 1967, at the Ebenezer Baptist Church in Atlanta, "Now the judgement of God is upon us, and we must either learn to live together as brothers or we are all going to perish together as fools."

King was assassinated on April 4, 1968, in Memphis, Tennessee.

Seth Luther

Born in 1799, carpenter Seth Luther became a valuable member of the early labor movement as a result of his pamphlets and speeches advocating labor reform. He reported that he received little schooling and learned from newspapers, books, and observations made during an extensive tour of fourteen American states. In 1834, the General Trades Convention in Boston selected him as one of their secretaries, and a year later he helped draft a manifesto known as the Boston Circular, which advocated a ten-hour workday. Workers in Philadelphia reprinted this pamphlet, which inspired a general strike against working conditions in at least one factory. In addition, as a result of Luther's efforts, the nation's first child labor law was enacted in Massachusetts in 1842.

Luther died in 1846.

Nelson Mandela

Nelson Mandela was born in rural South Africa in 1918. In 1942, while studying in Johannesburg, he entered politics by joining the African National Congress (ANC), an organization that sought to establish social and political rights for blacks. In 1944 Mandela and several friends formed the Congress Youth League (CYL), a subgroup of the ANC, which adopted a platform of nonviolent protest against South Africa's racist legal structure. This system, known as apartheid (apartness), subjected blacks to discrimination in housing, employment, and economic opportunity; denied them the right to vote; and imposed various other restrictions. The CYL's protests provoked violent responses from the South African government. In 1952 Mandela himself was beaten, arrested, jailed, and forced to resign from the ANC. However, he continued in his struggle against apartheid.

In 1960, in the wake of the Sharpeville massacre during which police killed sixty-nine unarmed demonstrators in a suburb of Johannesburg, Mandela was detained and the ANC was banned. Mandela decided that the nonviolent approach was proving ineffective, so he decided on more extreme tactics. Umkhonto we Sizwe (MK), the military wing of the ANC, was born in 1961. Under Mandela's leadership it launched a campaign of sabotage against government and economic installations.

In 1962 Mandela left the country for military training in Algeria and to arrange training for other MK members. On his return he was arrested for leaving the country illegally and for incitement to strike. He conducted his own defense and was convicted and jailed for five years in November 1962. While serving his sentence, he was charged with sabotage and was sentenced to life imprisonment. In prison Mandela never compromised his political principles. During the 1970s and again in the 1980s he rejected the offer of freedom if he renounced violence. However, shortly after his release from prison on February 11, 1990, Mandela and his delegation agreed to the suspension of armed struggle.

Nelson Mandela was inaugurated as the first democratically elected president of South Africa on May 10, 1994. In June 1999

he retired from public life. He currently resides in his birthplace of
Qunu, Transkei.

Jean-Paul Marat

Jean-Paul Marat, born in 1743 to lower-middle-class parents in
Switzerland, practiced successfully as a physician for several years.
He eventually moved to Paris, published several books on philosophical and political themes, and established himself as a
spokesperson of the lower classes in Paris. He first earned recognition through the publication of his book *The Chains of Slavery*. In
1789 Marat began to publish his own newspaper, *L'Ami du Peuple
(The Friends of the People)*. His dramatic oratory increased his
popularity among the lower classes.

Although the French Revolution of 1789 had weakened the
power of the monarchy, Marat believed more radical change was
needed. In 1792, the revolution indeed took a more radical turn.
Marat was elected to the Convention, which was created to serve as
the French legislature for three years. He sided with the left-wing Ja-
cobin faction of the Convention in opposition to the more conservative Girondins. The animosity between these two parties reached
extreme proportions. The Girondins succeeded in having Marat arrested and tried, but Marat won his own freedom by means of a persuasive speech. He then went on to have Girondin leaders unseated
and arrested. In response, in 1793, Charlotte Corday, a conservative
Girondin, murdered Marat in his bathtub with a knife. Marat's popularity during his lifetime was only outmatched by his popularity
following his death. He became known throughout France as a martyr for the cause of the freedom of the people.

Karl Marx

Karl Marx was born in Germany in 1818. He studied law and philosophy in Bonn and at the University of Berlin. After completing
his studies, he spent time in Paris and Brussels. In Brussels, he
founded the German Workers' Party and was active in the Communist League. In 1848, with his friend and collaborator Friedrich
Engels, he published *The Communist Manifesto*. After being ex-
pelled from France, Brussels, and Germany for his radical views, in
1849 Marx moved to London, where he remained in exile the rest
of his life. He worked as a journalist from 1852 to 1862. In 1864
he helped form the International Workingmen's Association. However, he dissolved this organization in 1872 to keep it from falling
under the leadership of anarchists.

Marx was the author of hundreds of articles, brochures, and reports, but he published only five books during his lifetime, including *Das Kapital*, the first volume of which appeared in 1867. Central to his philosophy was the notion that capitalism would eventually give way (after a class struggle) to communism—a classless society without inequality or exploitation. Marx's ideas, although relatively obscure during his lifetime, had a tremendous impact on future generations and formed the foundations of socialist and Communist movements around the world.

Marx died in his armchair in London on March 14, 1883.

Red Jacket (Sagoyewatha)

Red Jacket was born into the Wolf clan of the Seneca tribe, the largest of six tribes to make up the Iroquois Confederation. The exact date of his birth is unknown, but most historians agree that he was born between 1756 and 1758. Upon becoming chief of the tribe, he was given the name Sagoyewatha, which means "He Keeps Them Awake." He became known as Red Jacket as a result of the many red coats he wore while he supported the British during the Revolutionary War.

Although some Indians accused Red Jacket of being a coward in battle, he demonstrated unmistakable skill as an orator and as a negotiator. He served as chief of the Seneca tribe and as a leader of the Iroquois Confederation from the 1770s until the 1820s. In this capacity, he represented Seneca interests at the New York land treaty negotiations of 1794 and 1797. Red Jacket strongly opposed the partitioning of Indian lands and the conversion of Indians to Christianity. Although in the early part of his career he met with President George Washington and supported the education of Indians in the ways of the white man, later in his life he advocated that his people maintain their traditional Iroquois beliefs. His temporarily successful efforts resulted in the expulsion of all Christian missionaries from the Seneca territory in 1824. However, he found himself caught in a battle between the Indian zealot Handsome Lake and the white and Indian Christian missionaries. Handsome Lake charged him with being responsible for the sale of Indian lands to the whites as well as with practicing witchcraft. Red Jacket successfully defended himself against the charges, which, if found to be true, would have resulted in his death. However, due to these accusations, as well as to his problems with alcohol, in 1827 he was deposed as Seneca chief.

In 1830 Red Jacket died at his tribal village in Buffalo, New York. His wife, who had converted to Christianity, had him buried in a Christian cemetery, observing the tradition of a Christian religious service.

Mary Robinson

Born in Ballina, County Mayo, Ireland, on May 21, 1944, Mary Robinson was educated at Trinity College, Dublin, where she received a master of arts degree in 1970. She also earned a barrister-at-law degree from the King's Inns, Dublin, and a master of laws degree from Harvard University.

At the age of twenty-five Robinson was appointed Reid Professor of Constitutional and Criminal Law at Trinity College and served as a lecturer in European community law. In 1988, with her husband Nicholas, Robinson founded the Irish Centre for European Law. From 1969 to 1989, she served as a member of Seanad Éireann, the upper house of Parliament, and also served on the Dublin city council and the International Commission of Jurists.

In December 1990 Robinson was inaugurated as the seventh president of Ireland. The Robinson presidency was characterized by a concerted effort to improve the situations of marginalized groups within Ireland as well as to draw attention to global crises. Robinson was the first head of state to visit famine-stricken Somalia in 1992 and also the first to go to Rwanda in the aftermath of the genocide there in 1994.

In June 1997 Robinson was appointed to serve as the United Nations high commissioner for human rights. She insists that pressures must be exerted on all countries, including UN member states, that violate statutes put forth in the UN Universal Declaration of Human Rights.

Eleanor Roosevelt

Anna Eleanor Roosevelt was born on October 11, 1884, in New York City. Her parents, Elliott and Anna Hall Roosevelt, were members of socially prominent families, and she was a niece of President Theodore Roosevelt. She had a difficult childhood. Her mother, known for her beauty, called Eleanor "Granny," and her father, whom she adored, was banished from the family due to alcoholism. On March 17, 1905, she married her distant cousin, Franklin D. Roosevelt. Eleanor gave birth to six children, one of whom died in infancy.

In 1918 Roosevelt discovered her husband's love for another woman. Eleanor and Franklin Roosevelt reconciled, and while Eleanor continued to support her husband's political career, she was determined to build a life of her own, becoming active in a number of political organizations. After Franklin Roosevelt was stricken with polio in 1921, Eleanor sought to keep her husband's interest in public affairs alive. Encouraged and tutored by Louis

Howe, Franklin Roosevelt's close adviser, she became her husband's political stand-in.

Roosevelt's husband became president in 1933, and as first lady she broke many precedents. She initiated weekly press conferences with female reporters, lectured throughout the country, and had her own radio program. In addition, Eleanor Roosevelt sought to improve the status of blacks, women, youths, and poor, marginalized segments of society.

After her husband's death in 1945, Roosevelt was appointed as a member of the U.S. delegation to the United Nations by President Harry S. Truman. As chairman of the Commission on Human Rights, she was instrumental in the drafting of the UN Declaration of Human Rights. She resigned from the United Nations in 1952 but was reappointed by President John F. Kennedy in 1961. Roosevelt died the next year, on November 7, 1962, in New York City, and was buried in the rose garden at Hyde Park, New York, next to her husband.

Salman Rushdie

Salman Rushdie, born in Bombay, India, in 1947, grew up in the Muslim faith. However, he went to the mosque only a couple of times a year and never considered his family devout. In 1961 he was sent to England to attend the exclusive Rugby School. In 1964 his parents moved to the predominantly Muslim country of Pakistan, where he proceeded to spend his school vacations. In 1968 he graduated from King's College, Cambridge, where he majored in history. After his graduation he returned to Pakistan and settled down to write a play for television. The play was censored by authorities for containing the word *pork,* a meat that Muslims are forbidden to eat because it is considered unclean.

Rushdie returned to England following this incident due to his frustration with such restrictions. He began working as an advertising copywriter during the day and wrote novels during his free time.

Since the beginning of his career, Rushdie has written fantastical novels. In 1975 he published *Grimus,* a novel that tells the story of an American Indian who receives the gift of immortality. *Midnight's Children* is an epic about India's history since the end of British rule. Its hero, Saleem Sinai, is one of 1,001 babies born in the first hour of India's independence. The novels that have followed continue to mix history, myth, fantasy, and politics.

Rushdie is best known for the controversy surrounding his 1988 novel *The Satanic Verses.* This novel was considered blasphemous by many Muslims, and the Iranian ayatollah Ruhollah Khomeini issued a death sentence against the author. Rushdie has lived in hiding since that time, emerging only occasionally to make unannounced appearances.

Andrei Sakharov

Born in 1921 in Moscow, Russia, Andrei Sakharov became one of the Soviet Union's most brilliant physicists. Sakharov, with other prominent physicists, helped advance nuclear weaponry. In 1949 he worked on the research team that succeeded in testing an atomic bomb. However, Sakharov grew concerned about the negative effects of nuclear weapons on the environment.

In addition, he began to voice his objections to the restoration of Joseph Stalin's reputation in the country. Stalin was a controversial figure in Soviet history, for he had instigated the imprisonment and executions of countless Jews, political prisoners, and other ethnic minorities. In 1966 Sakharov, along with other scientists, addressed an open letter of protest to the Soviet Union's political leaders, expressing their opposition to reviving Stalin's memory.

In 1970, to help prevent future abuses of the Russian people, Sakharov organized and led a human rights movement to help educate Soviet citizens about their rights provided within the Soviet Constitution. During this time, he met another human rights activist, Yelena Bonner, whom he married in 1971.

Sakharov's reputation as a peace activist and as an outspoken Soviet dissident reached its height when, in 1979, he condemned the Soviet invasion of Afghanistan. As a result of his protest, the government sent him into exile. Relocated to Gorky, a city 250 miles east of Moscow, he became a virtual prisoner. However, he also became a symbol of ongoing human rights abuses within the Soviet Union. The Western press frequently reported on hunger strikes he made in protest of his enforced exile. Finally, in 1986, he was released from exile by Communist Party chairman Mikhail Gorbachev. His first statement upon his return to Moscow called for the release of all other dissidents. He immediately resumed his political activities and openly criticized certain policies of Gorbachev. Elected to Congress in 1989, he joined forces with Boris Yeltsin and other reformers to form an opposition group to the Communist Party within Congress.

Sakharov died in 1989.

Pierre Sané

Born in 1948 in Senegal and educated in France in business and economics, Pierre Sané went from working in business to the nonprofit world of international development. He has worked for the International Development Research Center, a Canadian international organization dedicated to helping developing countries build their scientific and industrial capabilities. In 1992 he was appointed secretary general of the human rights organization Amnesty International.

Daw Aung San Suu Kyi

Daw Aung San Suu Kyi was born in 1945. She is the daughter of a popular Burmese leader of the 1940s, General Aung San, and his wife, Daw Khin Kyi. She first made international headlines in 1995 following six years spent under house arrest by the government of Myanmar (known as Burma until 1980).

While she studied at Oxford and married an Englishman, Daw Aung San Suu Kyi continued to be influenced by her father's earlier political leadership. Her mother became seriously ill in 1988, and she returned to Myanmar to care for her. During this time, the movement of opposition to the Burma Socialist Programme Party drafted her, and with essentially one speech, she became its leader.

Following the lead of human rights activists who came before her, Daw Aung San Suu Kyi organized peaceful, nonviolent rallies and demonstrations to oppose the controlling government. She became a leader of the National League for Democracy (NLD), a political party that opposes the military government currently in power. Placed under house arrest in 1989 because of her popularity among the Burmese people, she was told that she was free to leave her home in Rangoon, but only if she left the country and did not plan to return. At times she became quite ill from malnourishment. She often did not have enough money to eat. Communication with her husband, Michael Aris, who was still residing in England, was essentially silenced.

In 1990 the NLD became a political party and won an overwhelming majority (82 percent) in a national election. Nonetheless, Daw Aung San Suu Kyi remained under house arrest, and the military regime increased its repression of NLD by stepping up its efforts to imprison and murder its members.

Over the years, Daw Aung San Suu Kyi has continued her politically nonviolent resistance work, and her international stature continues to grow. She was awarded the Nobel Peace Prize in 1991, two years into her six years of enforced house arrest. She plans to continue her father's work to bring civilian rule and democracy to the country, and she hopes that countries in the West will pay attention to the human rights violations perpetrated on people in her country.

Sojourner Truth

Originally born a slave named Isabella Baumfree in 1799, Sojourner Truth was freed by the New York State Emancipation Act of 1827. She proceeded to support herself and her children by working as a domestic in New York City. In 1843 she became a follower of a self-proclaimed messenger from God and changed her name to Sojourner Truth. She believed that God had given her the mission of spreading the truth. For the rest of her life she traveled across the country preaching to and drawing large crowds in the cause of Christianity, women's rights, and abolitionism. Frequently white women would attempt to prevent her from speaking at their events in fear that she would frighten people away. Nontheless, her determination and popularity prevailed.

After the outbreak of the Civil War, Sojourner Truth raised money to purchase gifts for soldiers and distributed them to the camps herself. She also helped African Americans who had escaped to the North and were in need of shelter. She retired to Battle Creek, Michigan, where she died in 1883.

Rigoberta Menchú Tum

Rigoberta Menchú Tum was born in 1959 to a Mayan Indian family in Guatemala. Guatemala suffered from a civil war that lasted from 1960 until 1996. Her family was suspected of involvement in guerrilla activities, and her father was imprisoned and tortured for allegedly having participated in the execution of a plantation owner. In 1979 Tum's brother was arrested, tortured, and killed. On January 31, 1980, her father and thirty-six other people were burned alive as they occupied the Spanish Embassy in Guatemala City. Soon thereafter, her mother was arrested, tortured, raped, and subsequently died.

After these events, Tum became increasingly politically active. She fled to Mexico in 1981, but she has continued to fight from afar against the opposition forces in Guatemala and to struggle for Indian people's rights. In 1992 she was awarded the Nobel Peace Prize for her efforts.

Wei Jingsheng

The Chinese dissident Wei Jingsheng was born in 1950 to parents who were high-ranking officials in the Communist Party. He now lives in the United States and teaches at Columbia University. Much of his adult life has been spent in Chinese prisons.

Wei Jingsheng took part in the Cultural Revolution and served in the Red Guard, a revolutionary youth group of the Chinese Communist Party, during the 1960s. He was arrested and imprisoned in

1967 after Mao Zedong decided to crack down on the activity of this youth group, which he had originally created. After his release from prison, Wei fled to the Chinese countryside. During this time he witnessed the brutal toll that the country peasants paid for Mao's agricultural modernization efforts. He became disillusioned with the political system, which was described as "the people's democratic dictatorship" but did not allow for a diversity of opinions. This diversity seemed impossible to him within a dictatorship.

Following this political awakening, Wei began to write "wall posters"—posters written and then posted in visible places so that many people could read them. Wei wrote the wall poster "Democracy: The Fifth Modernization" in response to the "Four Modernizations" outlined by Deng Xiaoping, the new leader of China. Deng emphasized that China needed to modernize in the fields of science and technology, industry, agriculture, and the military. Wei proposed the necessity of a fifth field of modernization: democracy.

Many Chinese citizens began to be influenced by Wei's ideas and saw him as a leader in the democratic movement. As a result of the content of this poster, the government arrested Wei for engaging in counterrevolutionary activities and sentenced him to a fourteen-year prison sentence to be spent in isolation cells and in labor camps.

In 1993, eager to gain the Olympic Games bid, China released Wei from prison. He refused to accept freedom unless the government returned letters that he had written over the preceding years but that had never been sent. These letters form the basis of the 1997 U.S. publication *The Courage to Stand Alone*. Once he was released, on September 14, 1993, Wei returned to his political activities. Those activities included a meeting with American officials to discuss China's human rights abuses. Five days after that meeting, both Wei and his assistant, Tong Yi, were arrested. Tong Yi wrote an editorial urging President Bill Clinton to ask for Wei's release. Six weeks after the editorial was published, on November 16, 1993, Wei was released and traveled to the United States to receive medical treatment of injuries incurred during his imprisonment. His release was seen as a major indication of improved relations between China and the United States.

Since then, Wei has been living and teaching in the United States. As a political exile he continues to fight for democracy and the improvement of human rights in his native land.

Elie Wiesel

Elie Wiesel, born in Sighet, Transylvania, on September 30, 1928, grew up the only son of four children in a close-knit Jewish community. Well-educated in Hebrew studies, he concentrated on the Hassidic sect of Judaism.

During World War II his village was taken over by the Nazis in 1944. At age fifteen he and his family were sent to the Auschwitz concentration camp. Separated from his mother and younger sister, he remained with his father for another year. He never saw his mother or younger sister again, and his father died a few months before the end of the war. Wiesel served time at three other concentration camps—Buna, Buchenwald, and Gleiwitz. Following the war, Wiesel learned that his two older sisters had survived.

Wiesel spent a few years in a French orphanage after the war. Eventually he studied literature, philosophy, and psychology at the Sorbonne. He became a journalist and wrote for *L'Arche*, a French newspaper. During this time, Wiesel met Nobel laureate François Mauriac, who encouraged him to break his personal vow of silence regarding his concentration camp experiences.

Since then, Wiesel has become one of the most outspoken survivors of the Holocaust. In 1958 he published part of his Holocaust memoir, *Night*. This book spoke of the horrifying experiences of Jews within the concentration camps. The success of *Night* led Wiesel to write nearly forty other works dealing primarily with Judaism, the Holocaust, and the overall fight for morality amongst the races.

Since 1976 Wiesel has served as the Andrew Mellon Professor of Humanities at Boston University. President Jimmy Carter appointed Wiesel chairman of the U.S. Holocaust Memorial Council in 1978. In 1985 Wiesel was awarded the Congressional Gold Medal of Achievement, and a year later he won the Nobel Peace Prize.

Wiesel lives in New York City with his wife and son, Elisha, and continues to write and speak around the world.

Chronology

1215
Britain's King John is forced by his lords to sign the Magna Carta, acknowledging that free men are entitled to judgment by their peers and that even a sovereign is not above the law.

1381
The English Peasants' Revolt occurs.

1628
The British Petition of Rights is adopted.

1648
The Treaty of Westphalia ends the Thirty Years' War, which had split Germany into hostile religious camps; Europe reorganizes into a pluralistic, secular society of states.

1689
The British Bill of Rights is adopted; John Locke writes about the idea of natural rights of life, liberty, and property.

1776
The U.S. Declaration of Independence proclaims that "all men are created equal" and endowed with certain inalienable rights.

1783
The Massachusetts Supreme Court outlaws slavery in that state, citing the state's bill of rights, which states that "all men are born free and equal."

1785
The Virginia Statute of Religious Freedom, written by Thomas Jefferson, passes the Virginia House of Burgesses.

1787
The delegates of the Constitutional Convention adopt the U.S. Constitution; nine states ratify it the following year.

1789
The French Declaration of the Rights of Man and the Citizen is adopted.

1791
The U.S. Bill of Rights incorporates notions of freedom of speech, press, and fair trial into the new U.S. Constitution.

1807
The U.S. Congress outlaws the importation of African slaves into the United States; nevertheless, some 250,000 slaves are illegally imported between 1808 and 1860.

1815
The Congress of Vienna is held by states that defeated Napoléon; international concern for human rights is demonstrated for the first time in modern history; freedom of religion is proclaimed, civil and political rights are discussed, and the slave trade is condemned.

1830
Congress passes the Indian Removal Act in order to free land for settlement, forcing seventy thousand Cherokee Indians to relocate during what came to be known as the Trail of Tears; many Native Americans died on the long treks westward.

1833
Great Britain passes the Abolition Act, ending slavery in the British Empire.

1841
Russia, France, Prussia, Austria, and Great Britain sign the Treaty of London, abolishing slavery.

1848
Over two hundred women and men meet in Seneca Falls,

New York, to draft a bill of rights outlining the social, civil, and religious rights of women.

1863
On January 1, U.S. president Abraham Lincoln issues the Emancipation Proclamation.

1865
The Thirteenth Amendment to the U.S. Constitution, abolishing slavery in the United States, takes effect on December 18.

1868
The Fourteenth Amendment to the U.S. Constitution is ratified on July 28; the amendment prohibits abridgment of citizenship rights and reaffirms the principles of due process and equal protection of the law for persons born or naturalized in the United States and subject to the laws thereof.

1870
The Fifteenth Amendment to the Constitution, which states that "the right of citizens of the United States to vote shall not be denied or abridged by the United States or by any State on account of race, color, or previous condition of servitude," goes into effect on March 30.

1914
The Great War (World War I) begins; with new weapons, civilian populations become victims of expanded warfare; as a reaction, a new sense of international morality begins to emerge.

1919
At end of World War I, the Treaty of Versailles requires that Kaiser Wilhelm II be placed on trial for a "supreme offense against international morality and the sanctity of treaties"; he escapes, but for the first time in history nations seriously consider imposing criminal penalties on heads of state for violations of fundamental human rights; the International Labour Organization (ILO) is established to advocate human rights represented in labor law, encompassing concerns such as employment discrimination, forced labor, and worker safety.

1920
The League of Nations Covenant requires members to "endeavor to secure and maintain fair and humane conditions of labor for men, women and children, . . . secure just treatment of the native inhabitants of territories under their control, . . . and take measures for the prevention and control of disease"; the Nineteenth Amendment to the U.S. Constitution, granting women the right to vote, is ratified on August 26.

1924
The Snyder Act, approved by the U.S. Congress, admits all Native Americans born in the United States to full U.S. citizenship.

1926
The Geneva Conference passes the Slavery Convention.

1933
Adolf Hitler's Nazi regime comes to power in Germany on January 30, 1933.

1934
The U.S. Congress passes the Indian Reorganization Act, which restores tribal ownership of reservation lands and establishes a credit fund for land purchases by Native Americans.

1939
Germany invades Poland thus beginning the World War II.

1939–1945
During World War II, 6 million European Jews are exterminated by Hitler's Nazi regime; millions of other civilians are forced into concentration camps, and are subjected to "medical" experiments, starvation, brutalization, and murder.

1941
U.S. president Franklin D. Roosevelt, in a speech before the U.S. Congress, identifies four freedoms as essential for all people: freedom of speech and religion and freedom from

want and fear; Roosevelt and British prime minister Winston Churchill adopt the Atlantic Charter.

1942
Following the attack on the United States by Japan on December 7, 1941, the U.S. government forcibly moves some 120,000 Japanese Americans from the western United States to detention camps; their exclusion lasts three years; some forty years later, the government acknowledges the injustice of its actions with payments to Japanese Americans of that era who are still living.

1945
The United Nations (UN) is established; the Charter of the United Nations and the Statute of the International Court of Justice are signed in San Francisco; the charter states that its main purpose is to promote and encourage "respect for human rights and for fundamental freedoms for all without distinction as to race, sex, language or religion." Unlike the League of Nations Covenant, the charter underscores the principle of individual human rights; with the defeat of Germany, World War II ends.

1946
The UN Commission on Human Rights is established.

1948
The UN General Assembly adopts the Convention on the Prevention and Punishment of the Crime of Genocide and the Universal Declaration of Human Rights—the primary international articulation of the fundamental and inalienable rights of all human beings; the ILO adopts the Convention on the Freedom of Association and Protection of the Right to Organize; the Organization of American States (OAS) adopts the Declaration of the Rights of Man.

1949
The UN General Assembly adopts the Convention for the Suppression of the Traffic in Persons and of the Exploitation of the Prostitution of Others; the ILO adopts the Convention

on the Right to Organize and Collective Bargaining; the Geneva Conventions provide standards for more humane treatment for prisoners of war, the wounded, and civilians; the Statute of the Council of Europe asserts that human rights and fundamental freedoms are the basis of the emerging European system.

1950
The European Convention on Human Rights is adopted; U.S. senator Joseph McCarthy launches a vigorous anti-Communist campaign, charging, but not substantiating, treachery among the top ranks of the U.S. government; the U.S. Senate eventually condemns McCarthy for his conduct.

1952
The Immigration and Naturalization Act ends the last racial and ethnic barriers to naturalization of aliens living in the United States.

1954
The U.S. Supreme Court rules in *Brown v. Board of Education* that racial segregation in public schools is unconstitutional.

1955–56
In Montgomery, Alabama, Rosa Parks, an African American seamstress, refuses to give up a seat on a bus to a white man, which sets off a bus boycott; this successful boycott marks the emergence of the civil rights leader Martin Luther King Jr.; the case is finally resolved in the Supreme Court, which determines that Alabama's segregation laws are unconstitutional.

1957
The U.S. Congress approves a civil rights bill to protect voting rights for African Americans; it is the first civil rights bill since the Reconstruction period.

1961
The European Social Charter defines economic and social rights for member states of the Council of Europe; British lawyer Peter Benenson launches an "Appeal for Amnesty '61"

with the publication of an article, "The Forgotten Prisoners," in the *London Observer* newspaper on May 28; the imprisonment of two Portuguese students who had raised their wine glasses in a toast to freedom moved Benenson to write this article, which proved to be the genesis of Amnesty International (AI), a human rights organization.

1964
The U.S. Omnibus Civil Rights Bill bans discrimination in voting, jobs, public accommodation, and other activities; Martin Luther King Jr. wins the Nobel Peace Prize.

1965
A new Voting Rights Act authorizes the U.S. government to appoint examiners to register voters where local officials have made African American registration difficult.

1966
The UN International Covenant on Civil and Political Rights and the International Covenant on Economic, Social and Cultural Rights are adopted and opened for signature; together, these documents further develop rights outlined in the Universal Declaration for Human Rights.

1967
The UN adopts the Convention on Non-Applicability of Statutory Limitations to War Crimes and Crimes Against Humanity.

1968
The first World Conference on Human Rights is held in Tehran, Iran; the United Nations convenes member states to evaluate the failures and successes of human rights promotion since the adoption of the Universal Declaration of Human Rights and to work toward the elimination of racial discrimination and apartheid; Rene Cassin wins the Nobel Peace Prize.

1972
The U.S. Senate approves a constitutional amendment, the Equal Rights Amendment, banning discrimination against

women because of their sex; the amendment is later defeated for lack of sufficient ratification among the states.

1973
The UN adopts the International Convention on Suppression and Punishment of the Crime of Apartheid.

1976
The International Covenant on Civil and Political Rights and the International Covenant on Economic, Social, and Cultural Rights enter into force after sufficient ratification among UN member states.

1977
The United States signs the International Covenant on Civil and Political Rights and the International Covenant on Economic, Social, and Cultural Rights; a human rights bureau is created within the U.S. Department of State; its first reports on human rights are issued that year; Amnesty International wins the Nobel Peace Prize.

1980
The U.S. Supreme Court orders the federal government to pay some $120 million to eight tribes of Sioux Indians in reparation for Native American land seized illegally by the government in 1877; the United States signs the Convention on the Elimination of All Forms of Discrimination Against Women.

1981
The African Charter of Human and People's Rights is adopted by the Organization for African Unity (OAU); the UN Declaration on the Elimination of All Forms of Intolerance Based on Religion or Belief is adopted after nearly twenty years of drafting.

1984
The UN Convention Against Torture and Other Cruel, Inhumane, or Degrading Treatment or Punishment is adopted; Desmond Tutu wins the Nobel Peace Prize.

1985

The UN establishes the Committee on Economic, Social, and Cultural Rights and adopts the International Convention Against Apartheid in Sports; the UN Nairobi Forward-Looking Strategies for the Advancement of Women is adopted; the U.S. Senate votes to impose economic sanctions on South Africa in protest against the government's apartheid policy.

1988

After forty years of lobbying by nongovernmental organizations, the United States ratifies the Convention on the Prevention and Punishment of the Crime of Genocide (the "Genocide Convention").

1989

In Tiananmen Square, Chinese authorities massacre student demonstrators who are struggling for democracy; the UN Convention on the Rights of the Child and the Second Optional Protocol to the International Covenant on Civil and Political Rights, aiming at the abolition of the death penalty, are adopted; the Dalai Lama wins the Nobel Peace Prize.

1990

The Americans with Disabilities Act is signed into law, establishing "a clear and comprehensive prohibition of discrimination on the basis of disability"; the World Summit for Children adopts the World Declaration on the Survival, Protection, and Development of Children and of the Plan of Action for Implementing the World Declaration.

1991

Daw Aung San Suu Kyi wins the Nobel Peace Prize.

1992

The United States ratifies the International Covenant on Civil and Political Rights; a UN Security Council resolution condemns "ethnic cleansing" in Bosnia and Herzegovina and demands that all detention camps in Bosnia and Herzegovina be closed; Rigoberta Menchú Tum wins the Nobel Peace Prize.

1993
The Criminal Tribunal on the Former Yugoslavia is established in the Hague as an ad hoc international tribunal to prosecute persons responsible for crimes against humanity and war crimes since 1991; these trials represent the first international war crimes tribunal since the Nuremberg Trials following World War II; the UN agrees to establish a post of high commissioner for human rights; the UN General Assembly creates the post of high commissioner for human rights.

1994
The UN Decade for Human Rights Education is declared on December 23; an emergency session of the Commission on Human Rights convenes to respond to genocide in Rwanda; the first UN high commissioner for human rights, Jose Ayala Laso, takes his post; the United States ratifies the International Convention on the Elimination of All Forms of Racial Discrimination and the Convention Against Torture and Other Cruel, Inhumane, or Degrading Treatment or Punishment; the United States signs the Convention on the Rights of the Child.

1995
The Beijing Declaration at the World Conference on Women states, "Women's rights are human rights"; the Platform for Action designed at the conference contains dozens of references to human rights pertaining to women.

1996
Jose Ramos Horta and Bishop Bello win the Nobel Peace Prize.

1997
Mary Robinson, the former president of the Republic of Ireland, becomes the second UN high commissioner for human rights.

1998
The fiftieth anniversary of the Universal Declaration of Human Rights marks a cornerstone event in humanity's struggle to recognize, promote, and protect human rights and fundamental freedoms.

For Further Research

Collections of Original Documents Pertaining to Human Rights

NANCY COTT, ED., *Roots of Bitterness: Documents of the Social History of American Women*. New York: E.P. Dutton, 1972.

MICHELLE R. ISHAY, ED., *The Human Rights Reader: Major Political Writings, Essays, Speeches, and Documents from the Bible to the Present*. London: Routledge, 1997.

DIANE RAVITCH AND ABIGAIL THERNSTROM, EDS., *The Democracy Reader: Classic and Modern Speeches, Essays, Poems, Declarations, and Documents on Freedom and Human Rights Worldwide*. New York: HarperCollins, 1992.

WILLIAM SAFIRE, ED., *Lend Me Your Ears: Great Speeches in History*. New York: W.W. Norton, 1997.

ORVILLE SCHELL AND DAVID SHAMBAUGH, EDS., *The China Reader: The Reform Era*. New York: Vintage Books, 1999.

HENRY STEINER AND PHILIP ALSTON, EDS., *International Human Rights in Context: Law, Politics, and Morals*. Oxford, England: Oxford University Press, 2000.

DEBORAH GILLAN STRAUB, ED., *Voices of Multicultural America: Notable Speeches Delivered by African, Asian, Hispanic, and Native Americans, 1790–1995*. Detroit: Gale Research, 1996.

General Studies of Human Rights and Its Roots

ANN MARIE CLARK, *Diplomacy of Conscience: Amnesty International and Changing Human Rights Norms*. Princeton, NJ: Princeton University Press, 2001.

KERRY KENNEDY CUOMO AND NAN RICHARDSON, EDS., *Speak Truth to Power: Human Rights Defenders Who Are Changing Our World*. New York: Crown, 2000.

ROBERT DRINAN, *The Mobilization of Shame: A World View of Human Rights*. New Haven, CT: Yale University Press, 2001.

ANTHONY KENNY, ED., *The Oxford History of Western Philosophy*. Oxford, England: Oxford University Press, 1994.

OLIVER MENDELSOHN AND BAXI UPENDRA, EDS., *The Rights of Subordinated Peoples*. Oxford, England: Oxford University Press, 1997.

ALFRED GLENN MOWER JR., *The United States, the United Nations, and Human Rights: The Eleanor Roosevelt and Jimmy Carter Eras*. Westport, CT: Greenwood, 1979.

MICHAEL J. PERRY, *The Idea of Human Rights*. Oxford, England: Oxford University Press, 1998.

ADAMANTIA POLLIS AND PETER SCHWAB, EDS., *Human Rights: Cultural and Ideological Perspectives*. New York: Praeger, 1979.

JACK TOBIN, *Guide to Human Rights Research*. Cambridge, MA: Harvard Law School, Human Rights Program, 1994.

B. VAN DER HEIJDEN AND B. TAHZIB-LIE, EDS., *Reflections on the Universal Declaration of Human Rights: A Fiftieth Anniversary Anthology*. Boston: Martinus Nijhoff, 1998.

LUCILLE WHALEN, *Human Rights: A Reference Handbook*. Santa Barbara, CA: ABC-CLIO, 1989.

Specific Human Rights Issues and Background

SCOTT BARBOUR, ED., *Free Speech*. San Diego: Greenhaven, 2000.

CHARLES BLACK, *"A New Birth of Freedom": Human Rights, Named and Unnamed*. New Haven, CT: Yale University Press, 1999.

ALEX BORAINE, *A Country Unmasked: Inside South Africa's Truth and Reconciliation*. Oxford, England: Oxford University Press, 2001.

JOHN HOPE FRANKLIN AND ALFRED A. MOSS, *From Slavery*

to Freedom: A History of African Americans. 8th ed. New York: Knopf, 2000.

CRAIG KIELBURGER. *Free the Children: A Young Man's Personal Crusade Against Child Labor.* New York: Harper-Collins, 1998.

GEORGE LEFEBVRE, *The Coming of the French Revolution.* Princeton, NJ: Princeton University Press, 1976.

LEONARD W. LEVY, *Origins of the Bill of Rights.* New Haven, CT: Yale University Press, 1999.

KARL MARX, FRIEDRICH ENGELS, AND ROBERT C. TUCKER, *The Marx-Engels Reader.* New York: W.W. Norton, 1978.

ANDREA WOLPER AND J.S. PETERS, EDS., *Women's Rights, Human Rights: International Feminist Perspectives.* London: Routledge, 1995.

Biographies, Autobiographies, and Collections by Human Rights Leaders

DALAI LAMA, *Ethics for a New Millenium: His Holiness the Dalai Lama.* New York: Riverhead Books, 2001.

FREDERICK DOUGLASS, *Narrative of the Life of Frederick Douglass.* Mineola, NY: Dover, 1995.

LOUISE FISCHER, ED., *The Essential Gandhi: His Life, Work, and Ideas: An Anthology.* New York: Vintage Books, 1983.

MARY ANN GLENDON, *A World Made New: Eleanor Roosevelt and the Universal Declaration of Human Rights.* New York: Random House, 2001.

LOUIS R. GOTTSCHALK, *Jean-Paul Marat: A Study in Radicalism.* Chicago: University of Chicago Press, 1967.

VACLAV HAVEL, *The Art of the Impossible: Politics as Morality in Practice.* New York: Fromm International, 1998.

JEFFREY HOPKINS, *The Art of Peace: Nobel Peace Laureates Discuss Human Rights, Conflict, and Reconciliation.* Ithaca, NY: Snow Lion, 2000.

WEI JINGSHENG, KRISTINA TORGENSON, AND LIU QING, *The Courage to Stand Alone: Letters from Prison and Other Writings*. New York: Penguin USA, 1998.

JOHN PAUL II, *Crossing the Threshold of Hope*. New York: Alfred A. Knopf, 1995.

MARTIN LUTHER KING JR., *I Have a Dream: Writings and Speeches That Changed the World*. San Francisco: Harpers, 1992.

EDWARD LOZANSKY, ED., *Andrei Sakharov and Peace*. New York: Avon, 1985.

NELSON MANDELA, *Long Walk to Freedom: The Autobiography of Nelson Mandela*. Boston: Little, Brown, 1995.

THOMAS MERTON, ED., *Gandhi on Non-Violence*. New York: W.W. Norton, 1965.

SIDNEY PIBURN, ED., *The Dalai Lama, a Policy of Kindness: An Anthology of Writings by and About the Dalai Lama*. Ithaca, NY: Snow Lion, 1990.

DAW AUNG SAN SUU KYI, *The Voice of Hope*. New York: Seven Stories, 1997.

RIGOBERTA MENCHÚ TUM, *Crossing Borders*. London: Verso, 1998.

ELIE WIESEL, *Night*. New York: Bantam Books, 1982.

HAROLD WU AND CAROLYN WAKEMAN, EDS., *Bitter Winds: A Memoir of My Years in China's Gulag*. New York: John Wiley & Sons, 1994.

Index

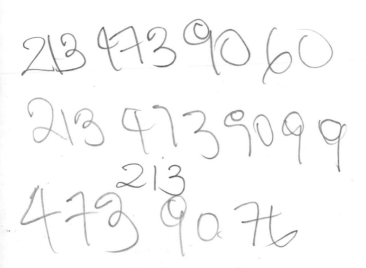